THE MILL GIRLS

The Newfoundland women who transformed Canada's industrial heartland

Heather Barrett

BOULDER BOOKS

THE MILL GIRLS

BOULDER
BOOKS

Library and Archives Canada Cataloguing in Publication

Title: The mill girls : the Newfoundland women who transformed Canada's industrial heartland /
Heather Barrett.
Names: Barrett, Heather (Journalist), author.
Description: Includes bibliographical references.
Identifiers: Canadiana 20250251426 | ISBN 9781989417614 (hardcover)
Subjects: LCSH: Women textile workers—Ontario—Cambridge—History—20th century. | LCSH: Textile workers—Ontario—Cambridge—History—20th century. | LCSH: Women textile workers—Newfoundland and Labrador—History—20th century. | LCSH: Textile workers—Newfoundland and Labrador—History—20th century. | LCSH: Textile industry—Ontario—Cambridge—History—20th century.
Classification: LCC HD6073.T42 B37 2025 | DDC 331.4/87700971344—dc23

978-1-998220-35-9 (ePub)
978-1-998220-36-6 (pdf)

Published by Boulder Books
Portugal Cove-St. Philip's, Newfoundland and Labrador
www.boulderbooks.ca

Design and layout: Tanya Montini
Editor: Stephanie Porter
Copy editor: Iona Bulgin

Printed in Canada

We acknowledge the financial support of the Government of Newfoundland and Labrador through the Department of Tourism, Culture, Arts and Recreation.

Funded by the Government of Canada | Financé par le gouvernement du Canada | Canada

For all the women who found the bravery to take a chance and follow their dreams

Table of Contents

1

The Photos

The black-and-white photos draw you in. The Hespeler Heritage Centre in Cambridge, Ontario, has them framed and hanging on the walls of their community-run archive and museum and loosely stored in cardboard boxes. These photos of young people, mostly from Newfoundland, in the 1940s, do not show them working in the fishery, on the battlefield, or struggling to survive in outport Newfoundland.

Hundreds of these square photos feature scores of young women in their teens and early 20s at work and at leisure in what could be a vintage North American college environment, but there are no obvious signs of academic life.

Ida stands on a verdant lawn, with a neat clapboard building and leafy bushes in the background, wearing coveralls and a cardigan, her braided hair piled on her head, the picture of casual chic. She's sipping from a straw in a soda bottle, and she's looking straight into the camera, a glint of mischief, even sauciness, in her eyes.

Ida Howse (married name Davis), shown here outside Winston Hall, was a mill girl from Newfoundland. Courtesy of Hespeler Heritage Centre.

A winter scene: An outdoor skating rink, buildings in the background. Helen and Gladys, wearing sporty winter jackets and warm baggy pants, skate arm in arm, scarves tied like bandanas on their heads, in animated conversation.

A girls' baseball team: some players kneeling, some standing, all wearing collegiate-style sweaters emblazoned with *DWW Shamrocks.*

And photos of dances. The young women wear well-tailored dresses, bright lipstick, and roller-set hairdos. They're dancing with young men, handsome in military uniforms, in full peacock mode.

Then there are photos taken in a cavernous industrial workplace. Workrooms so large the back walls aren't visible. The rooms are filled with mammoth, wrought-iron machines—huge, steampunk creatures—with wheels, pulleys, rollers, and metal teeth, ready to chew up something, or someone. Overhead lights dangle from the high ceilings; giant pulleys hold factory-sized spools of thread and wide bolts of cloth. Young women, clad in pants, overalls, or casual skirts, sometimes with headscarves, appear in most of these photos. Sometimes they are operating the machinery. In others, they are arranged, sports-team style, in front of equipment, occasionally with older male supervisors standing at the back of the pack.

Hundreds, perhaps thousands, of similar square black-and-white photos taken by Brownie cameras languish in storage boxes and photo albums in attics and basements all over southwestern Ontario and across Newfoundland and Labrador. Groups of young women and men, the girls in fashionable summer dresses or pleated slacks, the boys in white shirts with rolled-up sleeves and baggy pants, horseplaying in the park, going on automobile trips together in a souped-up Model T Ford, lounging on the lawn outside large residences.

Where and *when* were these photos taken? *Who* are these people?

The young women work in the Dominion Woollens and Worsteds Ltd. Mill in the town of Hespeler, now part of the southwestern Ontario city of Cambridge. The others are their friends, supervisors, surrogate family members, and local boyfriends and would-be suitors.

These young women kept that factory—the largest textile mill in the British Commonwealth at the time—going, during the 1940s, the years of World War II, and the peacetime years that followed.

Across Canada and in other British Commonwealth countries, young women took over industrial jobs that men had held before they signed up to serve in World War II.

This book is about one workplace—Dominion Woollens and Worsteds—and its life-changing impact on a generation of young Newfoundland women.

By 1945, about 5,000 young women had moved to Hespeler to work at Dominion Woollens and Worsteds.[1] Still more women came during the postwar years. Some were recruited from northern Ontario; others from Newfoundland, which, at that time, was a colony of Britain.

No one seems to have kept an accurate count of the teenagers and 20-somethings from Newfoundland who became "mill girls" in the 1940s. Community historians estimate that several hundred young Newfoundland women journeyed by rail, ferry, and rail again to Canada to work at Dominion Woollens and Worsteds and live together in the company residences during the decade of World War II and its immediate aftermath.

Few career options existed for young women in Newfoundland in the 1940s, if they weren't inclined toward teaching, nursing, or secretarial work or being a nun.

Newfoundland was a bankrupt colony of Britain. Its economy revolved around the fishery, with some forestry and mining thrown into the mix. Young, undereducated women in Newfoundland generally married early, had large families, and worked mainly in the family home, cooking, cleaning, and raising children, and perhaps growing a kitchen garden or keeping domestic animals.

The teenagers and 20-somethings who became mill girls chose something else.

They left their families and friends in Newfoundland and threw themselves into the great unknown, which for them was the southwestern Ontario town of Hespeler. They were not following a boyfriend, brother, husband, or any man. They went to take jobs at the gigantic Dominion Woollens and Worsteds textile mill.

This book is a testament to their bravery and adventurous spirits. This wasn't just moving two towns over: this was leaving family and going to a foreign country.

As Patti Nicholson, the daughter of mill girl Dolly Walsh, put it, "It's like [the film] *A League of Their Own*, but with mill workers instead of baseball players."

The mill girls from Newfoundland started a change that would shape Newfoundland—and southwestern Ontario—during the second half of the 20th century, one that sent thousands of young Newfoundland workers "up to the mainland" to manufacturing jobs in southern Ontario, a trend that continues today.

I first heard about the mill girls from Bernardine Stapleton and Nicole Smith, playwrights and performers who created *Girls from Away*, a play about these young women.

"It was more than just a demographic shift. It was cultural, it was financial, it was feminist, when they didn't have a word that said 'feminist,'" Stapleton points out. "Because they were behaving like feminists, even though there was no template for it at the time."

I created a documentary for CBC Radio about these young mill girls in 2021, and like Stapleton and Smith, I couldn't stop thinking about them.

Even in Newfoundland and Labrador, a province where people are deeply interested in their own heritage, the mill girls' story is little known. In Cambridge, they are a footnote to the early industrial decades of that city.

But a few people in Cambridge and Newfoundland and Labrador are dedicated to the mill girls' story. Lary Turner, executive director of The Company of Neighbours/Hespeler Heritage Centre, is one of them. Turner and his group are part of this story, too. So is Valerie Spring, a retired City of Cambridge employee whose 1986 graduate history thesis became an important documentation of the mill girls' lives.

St. John's-based Stapleton and Cambridge-based Smith, along with Cambridge folk musician Alison Lupton, are helping to spread the word about these women, too. So are the children, now older adults, of the mill girls whose lives are profiled in this book.

Hundreds of teenage girls and young women from 1940s Newfoundland took a leap of faith in travelling to a foreign country for jobs they had never before done. They started a youthquake in Hespeler that lit up the town with their Newfoundland saltiness, energy, and knack for finding adventures. At the time of writing, in 2025, nearly all of the mill girls have died. This book tells their stories through the generations who came after them in Cambridge and in Newfoundland, through their photos and memorabilia, their writings and recorded recollections, and through fictional vignettes based on real people. Step into the work shoes of these young Newfoundland women in the 1940s who were willing to take a chance on another kind of life.

Dolly

You never knew who you might see at the Newfoundland Hotel.

Dolly Walsh cleared dishes from the tables at the hotel's main dining room and its smaller coffee shop, where people watching was as good as at a concert, or at least at the cinema where her friend Olive Maher worked.

Posh couples from the wealthier parts of St. John's came on dinner dates, the women in furs and the men in woollen overcoats. Sometimes Dolly saw the same men come in one night with their wives, another with their girlfriends. She wondered if each woman knew about the other.

News announcers and copywriters from the Broadcasting Corporation of Newfoundland offices on the sixth floor came down to the coffee shop on their breaks, smoking and chattering about the reports they'd just read on the airwaves.

Sea captains from Portuguese and Spanish fishing schooners moored in St. John's harbour talked business over dinner with

Dolly Walsh (later Power) in a promotional photo for Dominion Woollens and Worsteds. Photo by Frank Johnston, courtesy of Hespeler Heritage Centre.

local merchants. Handsome military men from England and the United States swung by for drinks and sandwiches. The English men had exotic accents and drank a lot of tea; the American men had broad smiles, shiny white teeth, and booming voices.

As Dolly cleared glasses, plates, and cutlery from their tables, she made up stories in her head about their lives and what they did when they were not at the hotel. She imagined their stately houses, their important jobs. She wondered about the handsome soldiers' wives back home.

Dolly was particularly interested in the military men, so striking in their uniforms and shiny boots. In her mind, one of these days she would serve a cup of coffee to a tall, blond boisterous American serviceman and he would be overcome by her beauty. Then, with his brilliant, toothy smile, he would sweep her off her feet and whisk her away to his American hometown—perhaps New York City, or Hollywood.

Even if a soldier didn't sweep her off her feet, Dolly always kept her eye and ear open for opportunity. With guests from all over the world coming to the Newfoundland Hotel, maybe they had ideas for Dolly about how to get herself out of the hotel and into the great world beyond. Then she would be living the life she knew she was destined for, rather than dreaming about it.

2

Dolly of the Battery

Dorothy Walsh, better known as Dolly, grew up in the Battery, a part of St. John's that was more like a Newfoundland fishing outport than part of an urban centre. A neighbourhood of small wooden houses and fishing stages clinging to the rocky, steep crags of Signal Hill, the Battery overlooks the entrance to St. John's harbour. The "streets" were narrow footpaths. The area was prone to avalanches and landslides. Running water and indoor plumbing were distant dreams to the families who lived there; those basics wouldn't arrive in the neighbourhood until the 1970s.

Dolly was born in 1926, the third-oldest Walsh child, and the first-born girl. Her father, like most Battery men, was a fisherman. Her mother had her hands full feeding and caring for the Walsh family, which would eventually expand to 17 children.

The Walshes lived on Outer Battery Road. To get there required walking on a winding dirt road past the neighbourhood water pump, down a footpath, then down a narrower walkway. The Walsh house had two bedrooms and a large main room, which was mostly a kitchen. The outhouse was down an even narrower set of steps at the back.

Dolly's life was always a tight fit.

"The children were stacked like cordwood," recalls Patti Nicholson, Dolly's daughter. "Mom remembers sleeping four to a bed."

The Walsh family was like other Battery families of the 1930s. Dolly's father's fishing boat and wharf were just down the cliff from their small house. Dolly's mother kept the kitchen stove going day and night to feed and warm the ever-growing Walsh clan: "That's all Nan [Dolly's mother] did: cook, clean, and have babies."

But Dolly's mother couldn't do all that work by herself. Dolly, as the oldest girl, was pulled into service in that tiny two-bedroom house, doing whatever was needed to help her mother run the household.

Dolly enjoyed school but made it only to Grade 8. Then she was needed full-time at home to take care of her younger brothers and sisters. For all intents and purposes, Dolly was a deputy mother.

While Dolly changed diapers, scrubbed laundry, and kept her younger siblings out of mischief, she watched ships from all over the world—naval vessels, cargo ships, and international fishing fleets—steam in and out of St. John's harbour.

"I think Mom knew there was more out there," Nicholson speculates.

Dolly did broaden her horizons in her early teens. She convinced her parents to let her take a job at the Newfoundland Hotel, the largest and finest hotel in St. John's. It would bring in extra money for the family. The Newfoundland Hotel was a 15-minute walk from her home, but for Dolly, it was a world away. At eight stories, with a grand, two-storey lobby and staircase, ballroom, restaurant, and coffee shop, visitors were a few steps from beginning their luxurious vacations.

At the restaurant and coffee shop, Dolly bused tables and served customers, all the while sizing up the people that came to dine and stay at the hotel.

She waited tables for American sailors. She served cod tongues and flipper pies to sea captains from as far away as Portugal and Greece. She even met American singer Frank Sinatra, who stayed overnight at the hotel. Dolly had her eye on the future, one that did not include the Outer Battery.

"She was hoping she would meet somebody just to get out," Nicholson suggests.

One day, when Dolly was about 17, she was clearing a table in the hotel dining room when she heard a group of Canadian businessmen talking about recruiting young women for jobs. She stopped what she was doing, introduced herself, and asked questions. Shortly after that conversation, Dolly was offered a job at Dominion Woollens and Worsteds in Hespeler.

Not only that, Dolly made sure that her friends, sisters Olive and Irene Maher, were recruited to work at the mill, too. Olive Maher had left school at the end of Grade 3; she worked at a movie theatre in downtown St. John's and, like Dolly, dreamed of being swept away to another land and another life, preferably by an American serviceman.

Irene, Olive's older sister, was also up for an adventure. For all three teenagers, work at the woollen mill represented a way out.

But there was a hitch. At 17, Dolly was underage, and in order to go work in Ontario, she needed a note from the Walsh family's priest attesting to her good character and a note of permission from her parents.

The note from the priest was easy to obtain. However, permission from her parents was much more challenging. Despite the hard work and crowded conditions of the Walsh family home, Dolly loved her mother and father, and they loved her. Nicholson recalls Dolly telling her that her father was very unhappy with her desire to move to Canada to work, but he finally gave his permission.

In 1945 or 1946—Nicholson is unsure which year—Dolly and the Maher sisters boarded a train at the Newfoundland Railway Station on the west end of Water Street in St. John's for the long journey across the island to Port aux Basques, then onto the ferry to Nova Scotia, and then more trains, first to Toronto and then to Hespeler.

Dolly, Olive, and Irene were ready for the adventure.

Eileen

Eileen was peeling potatoes, again.

The Penney family of Humbermouth, in western Newfoundland, needed supper and Eileen and her older sister, Lillian, had to help their mother run the household. They had five younger siblings. Eileen's father worked long hours as an engineer at the Newfoundland Railway. He would be hungry when he got home from work.

Eileen thought potatoes were the most boring objects in the world.

All of Eileen's friends who still lived at home with their parents in Humbermouth were doing the same thing. Peeling potatoes, washing clothes, scrubbing floors. Teenagers living with their parents in 1940s Newfoundland had to earn their keep.

Eileen went to school to Grade 9, but that was enough time at the books for her. She wasn't cut out to be a teacher or a nurse. Besides, Eileen liked to be on the go.

She enjoyed berry picking on the barrens or being in the woods watching the boys snare rabbits. Eileen often took her younger brothers and sisters sliding on the snow-covered hills around Humbermouth—because, secretly, she enjoyed it as much as they did.

Even cleaning someone else's house, especially a fancy house in nearby Corner Brook, brought interest to her day. It was always eye-opening to see what needed dusting in wealthier families' parlours.

At 18, Eileen had wrung every bit of excitement out of her life in Humbermouth.

Her boyfriend, Gordon Hiscock, had been away in the navy for nearly two years. Eileen knew he couldn't say much in his letters about what he was really doing. Whatever life was like on the high seas, Eileen imagined it had to be more interesting than the meal she was preparing or the load of washing she was hanging out on the clothesline. Eileen was waiting for something to happen.

Eileen had seen signs posted in the shops about a presentation at one of the church halls in Corner Brook. It was especially for young, unmarried women. Recruiters from a factory in Canada were going to be there.

Now that, thought Eileen, could shake up her week.

3

Eileen of Humbermouth

A 1944 photo shows Eileen Penney standing in her parents' garden, in front of low spruce trees, wearing a swingy pleated dress with a rib-knit sweater and a long, beaded necklace. Her dark hair is fashionably coiffed and a glint of mischief flashes in her dark eyes. The photo was taken just before 18-year-old Eileen left to go west.

Eileen, born on April 4, 1926, the second oldest of seven children, grew up in Humbermouth, at the mouth of the Humber River, next door to the booming pulp and paper mill town of Corner Brook.

Since the 1960s, Humbermouth has been a neighbourhood of the city of Corner Brook, but in the early part of the 20th century, Humbermouth was its own town, a station on the Newfoundland Railway and home to many railroad workers. Like many of the families in the town, the Penneys were a railway family.

The Penney family home was close to the railway tracks. As a railway engineer, Eileen's father was away a lot, travelling on trains that ran across the island of Newfoundland, from Port aux Basques

Eileen Penney in 1944, in her hometown of Humbermouth, Newfoundland.
Courtesy of Terry Gullage.

in the southwest corner all the way to St. John's, the capital city in the east.

While Eileen's father travelled, her mother took care of the family, raised the children, kept chickens and cows, and maintained a vegetable garden.

Eileen's dark eyes and hair and high cheekbones reflected her Indigenous heritage. Her maternal grandmother was Mi'kmaq. Thousands of fully and partially Indigenous people lived, and live, in western Newfoundland. Discrimination toward Indigenous people in Newfoundland was widespread.

"We never talked about it," says Eileen's daughter, Terry Gullage, a longtime Corner Brook resident, in her 60s in 2025. "People of Mi'kmaq descent had a really hard time getting jobs."

Even though no one in the family talked about their Indigenous identity, Eileen embraced hers through her connection to the land. She loved hunting, fishing, and spending time in the woods with her brothers.

Although Eileen didn't graduate, records show that she was in school until at least Grade 9, when she would have been 14 or 15 years old. Her daughter couldn't find any school records after that; it's likely her mother did not stay the extra year or two to complete her schooling.

Not finishing school, if you were a young man in Humbermouth, wasn't much of a problem. Work was available at the Bowater Pulp and Paper Mill in Corner Brook or in supporting the mill by cutting trees and bringing the lumber for processing. Boys and men also hunted and fished. In other words, young males—educated or not—were in a position to earn enough money to support a family.

By the time Eileen left school, World War II had brought the American military to the west coast. The Americans had built an airbase in nearby Stephenville, which employed many local men and women, in support jobs. It was generally accepted that the Americans didn't hire local people that they suspected of being of Indigenous descent.

A young female in western Newfoundland could find employment as a maid, housekeeper, childminder "in service" to higher-class families in Corner Brook, or shop clerk. None of those paid enough for a female to live independently or could be considered a career.

"The option for most women was to stay with the family until you met somebody and got married," Gullage points out. "I mean, that was your life, basically."

Eileen had always worked hard at home: cooking, cleaning, taking care of her younger brothers and sisters, tending to the cow and chickens, and tending to the family's vegetable plot, which was in another part of Humbermouth.

For someone who liked fun and mischief, this wasn't the most exciting way of life.

Eileen also missed her boyfriend, Gordon Hiscock. They had been going steady for several years. At 17, Gordon had followed in his two older brothers' footsteps and gone overseas, serving in World War II with the Canadian navy as a radar operator on corvettes. Eileen and Gordon exchanged letters when they could, and Eileen followed news of the war and Newfoundlanders' efforts closely.

Gordon Hiscock in his navy years. Courtesy of Terry Gullage.

And so it was that Eileen was especially interested in a recruitment session in Corner Brook presented by officials from Dominion Woollens and Worsteds.

"I think that she wanted to do something for the war effort," explains Gullage. "And of course, the Dominion Woollen mills were making [military] uniforms. Dad had been, by that time, in the navy for two years, and a lot of people here in Newfoundland were in the armed forces. And so she, I guess, felt that she should be able to do something, too. And ... my father's sister was in the WAAC [Women's Army Auxiliary Corps] ... maybe she felt ... why couldn't she do something as well? When this opportunity came up, Mom thought, 'Well, this is one way to earn a bit of money on my own and get away from all this work that I don't really want to do.'"

Ella

That's the last time I'm going to travel anywhere for a man, thought Ella.

Things were not going well between Ella and her boyfriend from Curling. Ella was living at her older sister's house in nearby Corner Brook, minding her nieces and nephews while her sister recovered from surgery, and regretting her move to Newfoundland's west coast.

Ella wasn't interested in school. She wasn't one for getting married and settling down right away in her hometown of Carbonear either. Ella had moved to St. John's on her own and found work at the tobacco factory and then the infirmary. Nothing fancy, but it paid for her room and board. Her move to Corner Brook had been a leap of faith that had fallen a bit short. After a few years of independence, moving into her sister's house and housekeeping and childminding in Corner Brook was as dull as the dishwater Ella faced right now.

Ella fed the children supper, brought broth and bread upstairs to her bedridden sister, and was cleaning up the kitchen.

But first Ella cranked up the radio in the front room.

Ella knew that her sister only turned on VOWN after the supper dishes had been cleared away and when everyone could sit in the front room to listen. But her sister was upstairs.

That's when Ella heard the advertisement.

"If you are a young unmarried lady, have you thought of working abroad? Mr. Wiener of Dominion Woollens and Worsteds of Hespeler, Ontario, Canada, will be in Corner Brook for a presentation tomorrow night. Learn about a day in the life of a mill girl, and find out how YOU can sign up!"

4

Ella of Carbonear

Ella Powell's family liked to be on the move.

"My Aunt Isabelle used to say they were go-getters," says Dale Bechtel, Ella's son. A journalist and broadcaster, Bechtel sat down with his parents in their later years and recorded lengthy interviews about their lives. He recorded Ella's story in the summer of 2004, when she was 78 years old.

Ella was born on September 24, 1925, in Carbonear, a booming fishing and port town in Conception Bay, on the east coast of Newfoundland.

Unlike many families in Carbonear, the Powells had not been there for generations. Ella's father, Herbert, was from a family who had come across the Atlantic from Wales, and her mother, Bethana, was from Labrador. Herbert and Bethana had met in Carbonear; they married and made their home in the house next door to his parents.

The Powells fell into the rhythms of life in the bustling outport town.

Herbert Powell, like many men in Carbonear, worked away. Carbonear harbour was the home port for busy schooners and their crews. Ships sailed from there to fishing grounds on the Labrador coast for months at a time, and other ships ferried salt cod from Carbonear to New England, the Caribbean, and Europe.

Herbert first fished on schooners that spent the summer months in Labrador, then, later, he worked as a cook on schooners that sailed farther afield. Family lore has it that one of the schooners he was on was sunk by a U-boat off the coast of Spain and all the crew escaped alive.

Having fathers away from home for months at a time for work was normal for families in Carbonear in the 1930s and 1940s. Once Herbert came home after a long time away and he didn't recognize Ella because she had grown so much in the interim. Despite her father's being away much of the time, Ella's childhood was happy. She had eight brothers and sisters. Her grandparents on the Powell side lived nearby, and the Powell children ran back and forth between the houses.

The girls picked blueberries and partridgeberries and sold them for 15 cents a gallon. During early summer, when capelin washed up on local beaches, the Powell children helped their father catch them in hand nets, then smoke and dry them. The family kept some of the preserved capelin for their own food supply and sold the rest.

Ella particularly enjoyed tending to vegetables that the family stored for the winter months, an activity she continued all her life.

Even the family's two cats pitched in, providing rodent control for their storage rooms.

Ella Powell outside a church in Hespeler. Courtesy of Dale Bechtel.

Ella and her siblings loved to play hide and seek, and she and her sisters played "tiddly" with sticks and stones, a game still played in Carbonear and other Newfoundland communities.

The Powell family's industrious nature paid off. Despite the hard economic times that fell on most of Newfoundland during the 1930s and the rationing during World War II, the family lived modestly but comfortably.

"Porridge for breakfast; Monday was hash; Sunday, kill a chicken, boiled corned beef and cabbage," Ella said.

Occasionally, the family's self-sufficiency could be cruel. For the birthday dinner of two of Ella's siblings, her father slaughtered a goose—not just any goose, but Ella's pet goose. When Ella found out, she went behind the family's shed and cried. It's something Ella told her children about many times over the years.

"Dad would buy and raise a pig then have it killed, preserve it in salt in the storeroom," explained Ella. "My sister Grace's coat, if it was too small for her, Mom would rip it all apart, turn it all inside out and make it new for me. She'd make our underwear out of sugar sacks. I still have one that I bought for making tablecloths and I haven't finished it."

Herbert brought his children gifts from Boston from time to time. Ella remembered him returning from Boston with a small toy baby buggy for her and a slightly large buggy for one of her sisters.

The one thing that wasn't going well for Ella in Carbonear was school.

"She didn't finish school," Bechtel notes. "She didn't like it and

I guess then you had the option, with your parents' permission, to drop out."

"I got a prize for writing and I liked arithmetic," said Ella. "But I didn't like too much of the others [subjects]. I didn't understand a lot of the questions."

Ella may not have considered herself to be book smart, but she was resourceful.

"Don [Ella's brother] was a lot younger than me, and he didn't want to go to school," said Ella. "So I told Mom I'd teach him if they let me quit school, so they let me quit school ... I tried to teach him but didn't do too good."

Teenage girls who dropped out of school in Carbonear did not have many options. They could pick up housekeeping and childminding or help dry and salt capelin and cod during the fishing season. Most girls who left school and stayed around Carbonear married and started their own families.

That wasn't a life 17-year-old Ella had imagined for herself. She watched the Portuguese ships coming in and out of the port to pick up salt cod. Her brothers left for months at a time to fish "on the Labrador" on coastal schooners. Other brothers, who, like Ella, grew up making money to support the family, were taking chances and starting their own businesses. Ella looked up to her older brothers and was inspired by their fishing trips and entrepreneurial spirit.

In 1943, Ella set out for St. John's, several hours away by train. It was the thick of World War II, and with many of the men away helping with the war effort, women were needed to fill jobs in St. John's.

Ella worked in the Imperial Tobacco factory near Rawlins Cross, standing at a table and packing tobacco tightly into tins. The pay was low, but Ella had a war ration book and a rented room with a mattress. She was living life on her own terms. She had friends to socialize with and, aside from her factory shifts, her time was her own.

In 1945, Ella found a slightly better paying job as a nurse's aide at the city infirmary. The pay may have been better but there was more stress—she and the head nurse, Mrs. Maher, frequently butted heads. World War II was finally at its end and men who had served overseas were coming home. If convalescing, they spent time at the infirmary.

That's where Ella met a young man from Curling.

The relationship was tempestuous. Ella's boyfriend, who suffered war-related psychological injuries, was in and out of hospital, back and forth between St. John's and Curling.

By 1947, Ella Powell moved to Corner Brook, near her boyfriend's hometown of Curling. Their relationship was off and on, and to support herself, Ella lived at her sister's house, taking care of the household while her sister convalesced from surgery.

After several years of living on her own, Ella was open to trying something new. That's when she heard an advertisement on the radio that would change the course of her life.

"I heard on the radio that there was a Mr. Wiener down from Hespeler, Ontario, looking for girls to work in the Dominion Woollens factory because all of the men were still not back from overseas," Ella remembered. "And I thought, this is a good chance to come to Ontario."

Daisy

Daisy Nichols was having a hard time sleeping.

Her three younger sisters had crawled into bed with her. They were arranged head to toe, stacked like the logs floating up the nearby Humber River. She turned onto her left side and her face slammed into a foot; she turned to her right and a knee poked into her ribs.

It's not that Daisy didn't love her little sisters, but with 11 younger siblings, she often craved more space.

Daisy's home in Nicholsville was no different than most homes in that small logging town. Everyone had large families. Children scurried in and out through everyone's houses, through the fields and forests, and down by the river to fish.

Nicholsville adults were as busy as the beavers that occasionally dammed up the tributaries leading into the 74-square-kilometre Deer Lake. Loggers, the men supplied trees to the paper mill 54 kilometres downstream in Corner Brook. The women constantly cooked and baked bread—fuel that kept all these workers and their families going. Everyone pitched in: keeping horses, cows, and chickens and growing carrots, potatoes, and cabbages.

Daisy's four older stepsisters had already moved to homes of their own. Daisy was the oldest girl still at home, which made her the second in command, after her mother, Grace. As much as Daisy loved Nicholsville and her family, she itched to spread her wings—or at least spread out in bed without getting her teeth kicked out.

Daisy lay wide awake, crammed in among the three little girls. She was nearly 20 years old and not married. The work available to women in Nicholsville—raising children and running a household, growing vegetables and feeding the livestock—Daisy was already doing that.

Her friends and cousins encouraged her to attend a meeting with them the next evening in Deer Lake where a presentation was scheduled with recruiters from Canada who wanted to talk to young, unmarried women in the area about work. A different kind of work.

5

Daisy of Nicholsville

Daisy Nichols, by everyone's account, was a sweetheart. With her brunette hair, wide eyes, and a smile that lit up every room, it's no wonder that, when she worked at Dominion Woollens and Worsteds, she appeared regularly in the mill's promotional photos.

But before Daisy became a mill girl, she lived in a small community in western Newfoundland. Daisy was born on December 4, 1927, in Nicholsville, founded by and named after her grandfather.

George Aaron Nichols of Nova Scotia first settled at the inland spot on the west bank of the Humber River, near the mouth of Deer Lake, in 1872. A hunter, trapper, and logger, he started a pine-tree-cutting business. By the time Daisy was born, Nicholsville was home to a thriving logging industry, which first supplied local timber mills and then became a significant supplier to the pulp and paper mill in Corner Brook, which opened in 1925.

Nicholsville was not a typical Newfoundland community. It was not a fishing outport built in a harbour or a cove, filled with people

Daisy Nichols at work at Dominion Woollens and Worsteds. Courtesy of Hespeler Heritage Centre.

who worked on the sea. Nicholsville's several hundred people worked hard in the lumber camps, cutting down trees. As land was cleared, people farmed. Because Nicholsville was inland, it was sheltered from the cold ocean winds, and its warmer summers created better growing conditions than those in most Newfoundland settlements.

As Daisy's father was a widower with four children, Daisy had four older half-sisters. She was the first of 12 children born to her biological mother and father.

"People have said she was born to work," says Gail Hammond, Daisy's daughter, who lives in Cambridge, Ontario. "[Mom] had a happy childhood, lots of memories with friends, swimming and fishing and winter tobogganing ... And she has fond memories of her father, his horses and his pet owl, and how hardworking he was."

The Nichols family kept chickens and cows. They had a Newfoundland dog, and they had a vegetable garden. Daisy and her half-sisters were childminders for their younger siblings, and they helped in the garden or with the animals, doing whatever outdoor work the women of Nicholsville did when their men were away in the woods.

Despite the hard work at home, Daisy was outgoing and energetic, and she made time to have fun with her cousins and friends, but she didn't finish school. Hammond thinks that her mother went as far as Grade 10, because she was clever at math and had beautiful handwriting. That meant that Daisy would have stopped going to school at around age 14.

Young men who dropped out of school in Nicholsville in the 1940s went to work in the lumber woods or on one of the bigger farms, or they joined the military and served in World War II. But, for Daisy, staying in Nicholsville would have meant continuing to help her mother with the work at home, until Daisy married.

The Nichols family home was crowded, as were many Newfoundland homes at that time. Even though Daisy had her own room when she was older, her younger sisters always asked to take turns sleeping with her.

In large Newfoundland households, the older brothers and

Daisy Nichols (front) at work at Dominion Woollens and Worsteds. Photo by Frank Johnston, courtesy of Hespeler Heritage Centre.

sisters moved out as soon as they were old enough; with new baby siblings arriving, parents needed the space and the economic relief of the older children living independently by their own means.

Dominion Woollens and Worsteds recruiters spent considerable time and effort in western Newfoundland in the mid-1940s; likely Daisy had heard about the recruitment sessions from her friends in Nicholsville and had gone with them to a presentation at a church hall in nearby Deer Lake.

"I'm amazed at her bravery for doing it," muses Hammond. "Because, when I was growing up, my mom was a real homebody. For her to leave the comforts of her home in Newfoundland and come here, I think it was just an act of bravery."

6

Hespeler

With the establishment of American and Canadian military bases in Newfoundland in the 1940s, local young women met and socialized with soldiers their own age. The young men in uniform told them about their hometowns in Canada and America and about parts of the world they had just seen on their tours of duty. Teenage girls in Newfoundland realized that there were other ways to live.

Going to Canada to take a job in Hespeler was one way to see something of the world and a way to stay out of the kitchen, at least for a while.

In the 1940s, Hespeler was a picturesque and bustling town, with about 3,000 residents, nestled on the banks of the Speed River. That river snakes gracefully through the farmland of Wellington County in southwestern Ontario, from just north of Guelph, then down a valley toward the town of Hespeler, now part of the city of Cambridge, before merging with Grand River in the town of Preston, now also part of Cambridge.

Hespeler had comfortable homes for workers and their families, parks, schools, seven churches, and a public library. Young Hespelerites played sports in their spare time, and Hespeler became known for its hockey, football, lacrosse, and tennis clubs.[2] Life in Hespeler was prosperous, orderly, and pleasant—humming along comfortably like the well-oiled machines in its factories.

The town's founder, Jacob Hespeler, had settled in the area in the mid-1800s, noting the river's potential. The Speed River was ideal for 19th-century industry: not too wide and rough, not too shallow and tame. It was the perfect size on which to build a dam, which could then power a cotton mill. Hespeler's cotton mills led to a flour mill, a sawmill, and a woollen and cloth mill. Around all that industry, a town sprang up. In 1895, a railway connected Hespeler to larger cities and markets for its products.

In the second half of the 19th century, the Canadian textile industry was growing rapidly—not just in Hespeler—thanks to the technology of the Industrial Revolution and the availability of labour.[3] In Ontario, Quebec, and the Maritimes, manufacturing mills were built alongside rivers, which provided power, and near railway lines, which made it possible to transport raw materials and finished goods.

In the first few decades of the 20th century, the textile industry was the third biggest manufacturing industry in Canada, after iron and steel. Hundreds of large and small factories produced fabrics from cotton, wool, silk, and, later, synthetic materials such as rayon.[4]

Bolts of fabrics, from such manufacturers as Penmans, Patons, and

An aerial photo of Dominion Woollens and Worsteds, likely taken in 1944, showing the back of the mill. The Speed River is in the front of the photo; Queen Street can be seen at the back of The mill. Courtesy of Hespeler Heritage Centre.

DuPont, made their way to garment and dry goods factories in Toronto, Montreal, Winnipeg, and beyond. Whether it was silk panties, cotton bedsheets, or woollen business suits, most mass-produced textile items in Canada were sewn from Canadian-made fabrics.

The jewel in the southwestern Ontario industrial crown was Dominion Woollens and Worsteds in Hespeler. From its beginnings with Jacob Hespeler in 1862, the mill had changed owners and expanded several times, until the sprawling complex had become the largest textile mill in the British Commonwealth, and the town's largest employer.

By 1940, the mill spread out along the Speed River like Canada's largest bedsheet. Several large brick factory buildings, three to five stories high, occupied about 500,000 square feet, or about 46,000 square metres. Wedged between the long factory buildings and the river was a boiler room building, storage buildings, wool and cloth dyeing buildings, and a five-storey limestone water tower. The entire complex spread over about 6 hectares, or 15 acres. It was so impressive that Hespeler entrepreneurs sold postcards of the factory complex, stretching parallel with the river on one side and the railway line and Queen Street, Hespeler's main drag, on the other.

Dominion Woollens and Worsteds employed one-third of Hespeler's population. The company built and subsidized housing for its workers. During the Great Depression of the 1930s, the company kept a file on every family in the town, and mill managers ensured that at least one member of every family had a job at the mill. As Valerie Spring states, "the loyalty the company obviously felt to the town represents an intriguing element in the relationship of town to company. Town and company were inseparable; the mill was run and staffed by Hespeler people."[5]

Dominion Woollens and Worsteds and the people of Hespeler were intertwined like the weave in the bolts of worsted woollen cloth that it produced. After Canada joined Britain to fight in World War II in September 1939, Hespelerites and Dominion Woollens and Worsteds pivoted to support the war effort.

About 452 residents of Hespeler enlisted in the military. From the Dominion Woollens and Worsteds roster alone, 226 workers signed up. The mill also answered the call to serve. The Canadian government pulled Dominion Woollens and Worsteds, and many other manufacturing mills, into wartime supply service. The mill was to produce cloth for military uniforms, blankets, and tents.

By the end of the war, in 1945, the mill could "produce enough khaki to outfit a division of 15,000 men every week."[6] That intense increase in production to meet the needs of the Allied war effort required more workers. As men had volunteered to serve with the Canadian forces, the factories where they had worked needed to recruit, too. This became a national manufacturing industry problem. The Canadian government, upon examining the dilemma, decided that manufacturing jobs could probably be done by women, an as-yet-untapped labour force.

Through the National Selective Service, the Canadian government moved workers from underemployed parts of the country to places where they needed workers, such as Ontario and Quebec factories. Young single women were their preferred employees, followed by married women without children.

In 1941, Dominion Woollens and Worsteds began a recruitment drive for young female workers. By then, they were in competition with most other factories and manufacturing facilities across Ontario and Quebec. Dominion Woollens and Worsteds had to look farther afield for young female workers—to northern Ontario, and eastward. The Canadian government struck an agreement with the government of the British colony of Newfoundland to recruit young women for factory work in Canada.

In 1940, 850 people worked at Dominion Woollens and Worsteds, and by 1945, that number had ballooned to nearly 1,500.

The staff worked three shifts a day, six days a week, churning out bolt after bolt after bolt of woollen khaki serge. It was a patriotic feat of industrial production, and wartime Hespeler was thriving. In addition to its textile mill, it had an enamel-cookware factory, a washing-machine factory, and a hockey-stick factory. Its pleasing climate had cold, snowy winters, balmy springs, sunny summers, and crisp falls: optimal growing conditions for the farms that surrounded the town. The farm families supplied the town with produce and meat and bought their supplies in Hespeler.

If there was any challenge at all in Hespeler, it was a labour shortage at the mill. Company officials decided that the answer was to recruit more young Newfoundland women. But asking young women—teenagers, most of them—to leave their home country and their families to travel to Hespeler was a daunting task. Recruiters needed a plan with military precision to attract and retain workers to make military uniforms.

If recruiters were successful in their mission, Hespeler would be invaded by hundreds of young women from Newfoundland.

7

A Day in the Life of a Mill Girl

Recruiting expeditions for Dominion Woollens and Worsteds, whether they took place in the francophone areas of northern Ontario or in small towns in Newfoundland, had to be carefully tailored to suit each community that was visited.

Each recruiter had his own style. Some simply posted announcements of presentations in communities or placed advertisements on the radio. Others took a more direct approach.

Lary Turner, executive director of the Hespeler Heritage Centre, became friends with a retired Dominion Woollens and Worsted Newfoundland recruiter who let Turner in on his trade secret: "He would either hire a taxi or rent a car in one of the communities and drive around on wash day and look for women's undergarments hanging on the line. And when he [saw] some undergarments that indicated there might be some young girls living in the house, he would stop and knock on the door and talk to the head of the household and explain what he was doing and whether or not

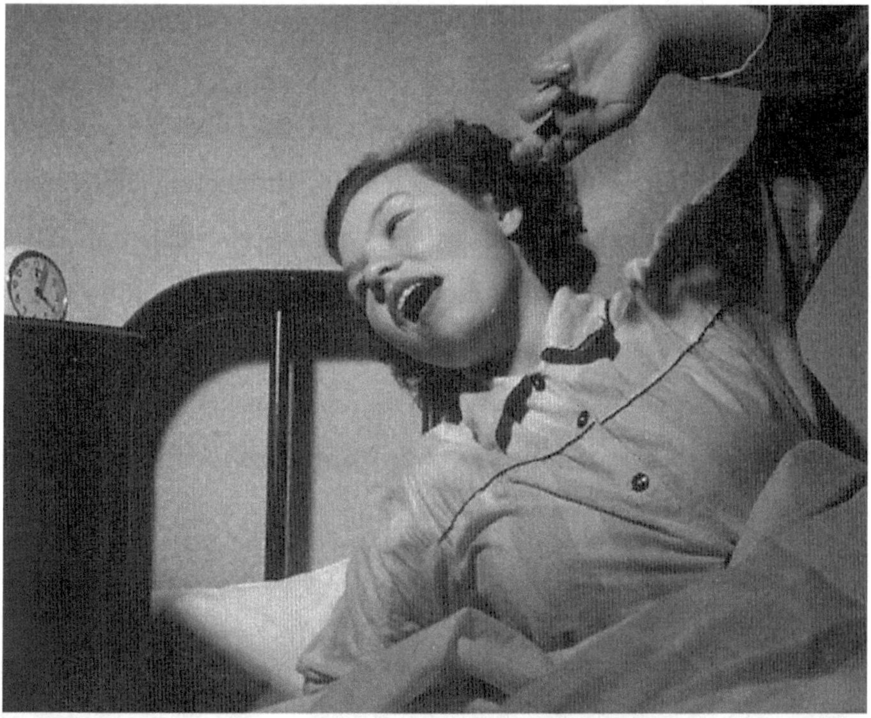

Betty Roscoe of Hespeler goes through the different stages of "a day in the life of a mill girl." Photo by Frank Johnston, courtesy of Hespeler Heritage Centre.

there was any young girls that were interested in working in far off Ontario. He recruited three sisters at one house like that."

In its peak hiring years in the 1940s, the mill had six recruiters working in Canada to hire young women, and several recruiters who focused on Newfoundland. Their efforts paid off. Between 1940 and 1950, recruiters hired about 600 young women per year, mostly from northern Ontario and Newfoundland.

Whether by radio or newspaper advertisements, by word of mouth, by stopping young women on the street, or by skulking around family clotheslines, reeling in teenagers and young women to their presentations at church halls and hotel meeting rooms was the first part of the recruiter's job. The second part required even more imagination.

When Eileen Penney, Ella Powell, and Daisy Nichols went to Dominion Woollens and Worsteds recruitment meetings in western Newfoundland, and Dolly Walsh sought out more information at the Newfoundland Hotel in St. John's, recruiters gave them, by 1940s Newfoundland standards, a modern, sophisticated pitch.

The recruiters didn't focus on actual mill work, or the salary, or even the patriotism of making military uniforms for the war effort. They showed the young women a slide show—*A Day in the Life*

Betty Roscoe at work at a machine in the mill. Photo by Frank Johnston, courtesy of Hespeler Heritage Centre.

of a Mill Girl—starring Betty Roscoe, an attractive young woman from Hespeler, who wasn't actually a mill girl but whose father, Bill Roscoe, worked there.

"They had this very glamorous starlet type of person who was actually from Cambridge, but she was cast as the girl from away," describes Bernadine Stapleton, a writer and performer from Marystown, on Newfoundland's Burin peninsula, who developed a theatre production about these young women. She has been fascinated by the lengths the mill recruiters went to appeal to girls who had grown up in rural communities, similar to the one she grew up in.

"You see her [Betty] waking up in her bed at the residence. And then there's another picture and she's brushing [her] teeth and she's got this toothbrush and toothpaste and the sink all to herself, and then you see her greeting her supervisor at the door of the mill looking like Greta Garbo in a suit. They [the mill girls] had their pictures taken a lot. We saw a lot of pictures that, like they're riding their bikes, looking very perky. They're getting ready for the dances ... Food played a lot into the recruitment. There were feasts; platters of fruit; pictures of food good enough for Top Chef."

The Dominion Woollens and Worsteds recruiters were well aware of what they sold to the young Newfoundland women.

"Recruitment was a pretty expensive undertaking," explains Turner. "Once you recruited a young woman, you needed to get her from wherever she was in Newfoundland to Hespeler. It was time-consuming. It was expensive. And once they [the recruiters] got a young worker there, they definitely wanted to keep her."

Woollen and textile mill work was noisy, hot, and physically demanding. Workers were expected to work at least 50 hours a week. Job turnover at textile mills was high; some workers, male and female, didn't last a year. Dominion Woollens and Worsteds learned lessons from A.R. Kaufman, an industrialist from nearby Kitchener, Ontario, who had recruited young women from Newfoundland a few years earlier, with less success. At the Kaufman mill, the young Newfoundland women found that being so far from home and working a demanding job was too much; many Newfoundland recruits to the Kaufman mill left shortly after their arrival in Kitchener.

Dominion Woollens and Worsteds determined that if it was going to recruit and retain young female workers from Newfoundland, and do it in a financially responsible way, they had to do it carefully.

Even at times of high worker availability, the turnover rate in the physically demanding textile industry was high. The companies constantly recruited. Dominion Woollens and Worsteds put the teenagers and young women who filled the hundreds of difficult, manual labour jobs on the factory floor in the centre of their public

Betty Roscoe reads messages on a bulletin board at the mill. Photo by Frank Johnston, courtesy of Hespeler Heritage Centre.

Back at the residence after her shift, Betty Roscoe makes a cup of tea. Photo by Frank Johnston, courtesy of Hespeler Heritage Centre.

relations campaign, showing them to be important enough to have the small moments of their daily lives extensively documented. They pitched recruitment as if it were a casting call for textile labourers.

For Daisy, Eileen, Ella, and Dolly, in addition to glamour the presentations showed them standards of living that would be unimaginable for them in their home communities.

If the young women took jobs at Dominion Woollens and Worsteds, the presentations showed, they would live in neat, modern multistoried residences, with older women on site to provide supervision and a safe, homelike environment. Their residence room would be shared with another young woman of the same age, and each would have her own bed. They didn't even have to wash their own sheets—maid service was provided. Platters of food, including a rainbow of fruit, food that they didn't have to grow or cook themselves, would be served to them. The bathrooms contained several toilets and uncrowded bathroom sinks where the mill girls could brush their teeth in peace.

Betty Roscoe on a regular visit to the company nurse. Photo by Frank Johnston, courtesy of Hespeler Heritage Centre.

That was all before they went to work. The presentation didn't actually show the young women doing the sweaty, physical work of operating the machinery, but it did show them standing by large pieces of machinery, a hand perhaps resting on a large, wrought-iron wheel, all while smiling for the camera. When the mill girls punched out of their factory floor shifts, they didn't even have to make their own fun—Dominion Woollens and Worsteds took care of that. The presentation included photos of organized dances at the residence halls with handsome young soldiers from a nearby Canadian air base. There were team photos of the girls who played on the company softball team and a company choir they could join. The company even arranged excursions to nearby towns and beaches.

"The mill really tried to keep them entertained," adds Turner. "It was a smart move economically, because if you have happy workers, they're going to continue to work there."

The presentation, tailored for girls and young women, showed a way of life that was about as far away from their current lives, geographically and culturally, as most teenage girls sitting in church halls in small towns in Newfoundland could imagine. They could become stars—of their own amazing lives—if only they moved to Hespeler to work at Dominion Woollens and Worsteds.

But becoming a mill girl meant embarking on a journey across the ocean, to Canada, a country of which they knew little. It meant adapting to another lifestyle and a foreign culture.

Their only contact with their families would be through letters. And, after travelling such a long, expensive distance, when could they return to Newfoundland to see their families again?

This would be more than a step. It had to be a leap of faith.

To that, Daisy, Eileen, Ella, Dolly, and hundreds of other teenage and 20-something young women from Newfoundland responded, "How do I sign up?"

8

Hard Working "Nice Girls"

If only it were as easy as signing up on the spot to become a mill girl.

Dominion Woollens and Worsteds needed young women in their teens and early 20s to meet the increasing demand for textiles. It recruited female workers in Newfoundland at about the same time that thousands of young people, mostly young men, had been recruited to join the military and help with the World War II effort.

Between 1930 and 1945, 2,889 Newfoundland and Labrador men joined the Canadian navy, one of them Eileen's boyfriend, Gordon Hiscock. From western and central Newfoundland, nearly 3,600 men had joined the Newfoundland Overseas Forestry Unit, working in the United Kingdom, to help rebuild infrastructure. Thousands more Newfoundland and Labrador men had joined the merchant marines. Still others joined the British Artillery or Air Force, and a few even joined with other Allied country military efforts.[7]

Even during peacetime in the first half of the 20th century, it was common for young men and boys in Newfoundland and

Labrador communities to travel for work. Ella Powell's father sailed on schooners to Labrador and to New England for months at a time. One of her brothers moved north to Labrador more or less permanently. Men and boys worked seasonally in lumber camps in Newfoundland's interior, like Daisy Nichols's father and the other men of Nicholsville did. Men and boys worked on the railway for weeks at a time like Eileen Penney's father did.

Men's work was often dangerous, as was military service. Some were killed on the job and others were injured in ways that changed the rest of their lives for the worse. But for most of the men, it was simply work. They went away to earn money to support their families or to support their country in the war effort. They came back with tales of friendships and adventures. Newfoundland families were used to their young men going away.

Newfoundland families were not, however, used to young women leaving so easily. Every now and then, young women moved away to work "in service" as domestic help in Canada and the Boston states, but most young women, including Eileen, Ella, Daisy, and Dolly, had several hoops to climb through.

After young women had seen the presentation at their local church or community hall, they were interviewed on the spot by one of the male recruiters dispatched to the area. As Spring describes this process,

> Recruiters had to be very careful in their selection of young women. Hard working "nice girls" were the first choice.

> The recruiter had guidelines to follow established by both the Company and the federal [Canadian] government as to who he was able to hire.... The women would be told of the type of work and the residences.
>
> In Newfoundland those women the recruiter was serious about hiring were given medicals. References were checked as thoroughly as possible. Recruiters usually met the young woman's parents to dispel any doubts they may have had.[8]

After the interviews, if recruiters thought any of the young women were appropriate candidates for mill jobs, they were sent off with paperwork to complete. Gullage still has some of the materials her mother needed to assemble to leave Humbermouth to go to Hespeler.

Eileen had to obtain a letter from the government of Newfoundland's Department of Home Affairs confirming that she was a British subject, native to Newfoundland. She needed another letter from the Newfoundland Constabulary in Corner Brook, a character certificate verifying that she had no criminal record and was of "good character."

But that wasn't enough. Eileen also needed additional character references: documentation that proved that she was, indeed, a "nice girl." Her letter, written by the local Anglican minister, Reverend T.E. Loder of the Church of St. John the Evangelist, dated September 16, 1944, states:

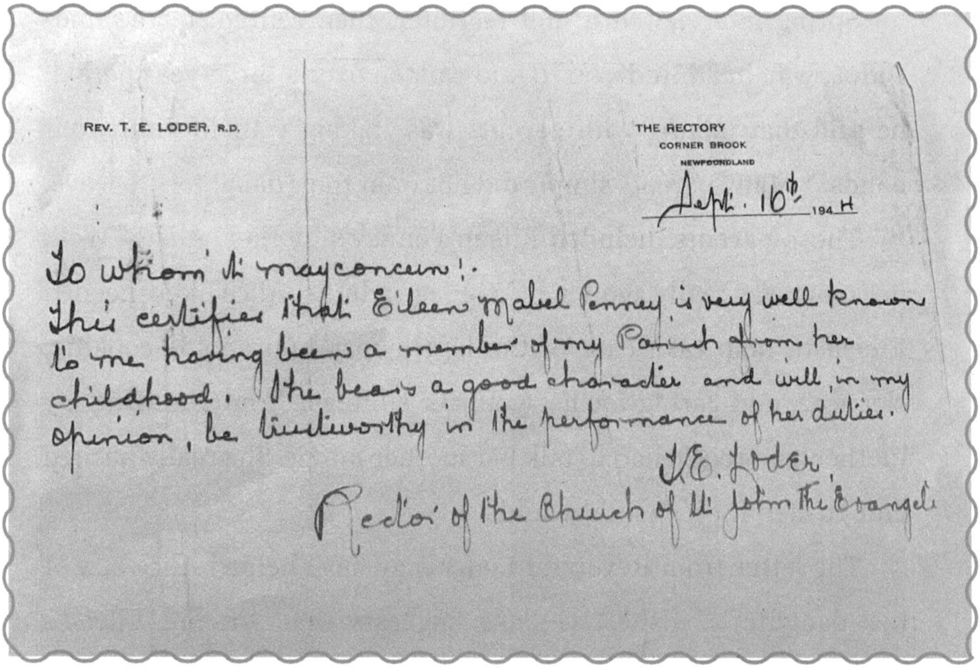

REV. T. E. LODER, R.D.

THE RECTORY
CORNER BROOK
NEWFOUNDLAND

Sept. 16th 194 4

To whom it may concern:-
This certifies that Eileen Mabel Penney is very well known to me having been a member of my Parish from her childhood. She bears a good character and will, in my opinion, be trustworthy in the performance of her duties.

T.E. Loder,
Rector of the Church of St John the Evangelist

A letter Eileen Penney had to obtain from Reverend Loder, attesting to her "good character." Courtesy of Terry Gullage.

> To whom it may concern,
> This certifies that Eileen Mabel Penney is very well known to me having been a member of my Parish from her childhood. She bears a good character and will, in my opinion, be trustworthy in the performance of her duties.

For many young women, including 18-year-old Eileen Penney and 17-year-old Daisy Nichols, the toughest hurdle was their parents. Because they were underage, they needed signed permission from their parents to go. The recruiters always met with the parents, and that meeting did not often go well.

Spring interviewed a mill recruiter, then retired, in the mid-1980s, who had hired 400 to 500 women over a three-year period; he said that talking with parents was "taking your life into your hands."[9] Many parents simply did not want their daughters to leave.

Those parents included Eileen Penney's mother, Alice. "Well, her mom was really against it," Gullage admits. Alice likely needed Eileen to help take care of the large, busy household—cooking, cleaning, and caring for her younger siblings. "And, knowing my mother, she *really* had to talk her mother into it. She really pushed and pushed for it," Gullage adds.

The letter from Reverend Loder may have helped Alice accept her daughter's wishes. Gullage suggests that Joseph, Eileen's father, may have understood that Eileen wanted an adventure and talked his wife into letting their daughter go: "He [Joseph] bought her a trunk, so that she would have something to take with her. And that was not a minor purchase back in those days."

Meanwhile, in Nicholsville, Daisy Nichols waged her own campaign. "She was the firstborn for her mom and she was young when she wanted to leave home, 17 or 18," points out Daisy's daughter. "It was a big step for your child to move that far away."

By the time Daisy had met with mill recruiters, it was 1947, and World War II was over. However, Dominion Woollens and Worsteds was still short-staffed and still recruiting young women in central and western Newfoundland. Daisy had compiled character references, medical clearances, and the necessary identification from the Government of Newfoundland. In the end, Daisy simply forged her mother's signature on the necessary paperwork.

For Ella Powell, the process was different. In 1944, she was 22 years old, a legal adult, and when she decided that she wanted to take the job in Hespeler, she did not need parental permission. According to Bechtel, "The person from Dominion said, 'Well you can make up your own mind, you're an adult now.' So I think it was an opportunity for her, and I don't think she saw a lot of opportunities in Newfoundland. I think my mother saw in her brothers that they could go often and do things that they wanted to do, so it must have influenced her decision to come up to Ontario."

All that Dolly Walsh's daughter Patti Nicholson knows is that Dolly's father was not happy. If Dolly left, that would mean that the next oldest girl in the family would have to take on Dolly's work in the home. Still, he gave his permission, reluctantly. Dolly assembled all her documents, including the all-important letter from her parish priest attesting to her good character. Dolly's departure also gave her younger sisters the same idea, as at least two of them eventually followed in Dolly's footsteps and moved to Ontario for work.

Between 1940 and 1950, the company recruited more than 6,000 people. How many were women, and how many from Newfoundland, is unknown.

"When you think about where [the company] was recruiting ... for these small communities, these villages, and towns to lose even five women to the recruitment would have a significant impact on the towns they were leaving behind," Spring notes.

9

The Trip

Eileen, Daisy, Dolly, and Ella were cleared for transportation to Hespeler. But how would they get to their new jobs, 2,500 kilometres away?

"Recruitment was a pretty expensive undertaking," Spring explains. "Once you recruited a young woman, you needed to get her from wherever she was in Newfoundland to Hespeler. It was time consuming. It was expensive."[10]

Young men in Newfoundland were frequently on the move—they walked, they hitchhiked, they took trains, boats, and, on rare occasions, their own automobiles to get to military enlistment, to jobs in Canada and the United States, and sometimes just to get away. But hundreds of young unmarried Newfoundland women travelling on their own to another country, on a journey that would take several days, was different. The young women would need to sleep on trains and ferries, and, possibly, in hotels. To their parents, to their clergy, and to their communities, the idea of these girls doing this on their own didn't seem proper. Opportunities for these "hard working 'nice girls'" to get tangled up in activities that weren't nice abounded.

Dominion Woollens and Worsteds had already thought of that. They had to assure parents that the journey would be safe. As part of the recruitment process, recruiters hired female chaperones to accompany the young women from Newfoundland to Hespeler. This long, expensive journey to their new lives was made more expensive by the addition of chaperones.

"Their transportation was paid by the employer, but they [the mill girls] had to remain for six months. And if they didn't stay there for six months, they had to repay the cost of the transportation," says Gullage.

Dominion Woollens and Worsteds would pay for the young women's travel up front, but the cost of the trip would be deducted from their paycheques for the first six months of their employment.

"I think she [Eileen] was very brave to leave," Gullage admits.

Eileen didn't board the train alone; at least one cousin was with her. Neither did Dolly. Dolly's friends, the Maher sisters, travelled with her all the way from St. John's. At the Newfoundland Railway station in Deer Lake, Daisy Nichols was buzzing with excitement; she also had at least one cousin with her.

St. John's. Deer Lake. Corner Brook. Port aux Basques. Then the ferry to North Sydney, Nova Scotia. "[Daisy] was extremely ill on the ferry crossing over, and because of that, she never went back to Newfoundland by ferry. She went back numerous times, but she always flew," says Hammond.

Back on a train at North Sydney, then another short ferry ride to mainland Nova Scotia. Then by train to Montreal. Toronto. Galt. Hespeler.

> The following young ladies left on November 17 for Hespeler, Ontario, where they will be employed by the Dominion Woollen Mills; Miss Edna Mildred Reid of Bishop's Falls; Miss Vera A. Pope of Badger; Miss Edna M. Elliott of Botwood; Misses Nora H. Pinsent and Louise Peckford of Buchans; Misses Constance M. Hiscock, Margaret McDonald, Miss Blanch L. Forsey, and Pearl Lander of Grand Falls; Miss Clara M. Green of Windsor; Miss Mary Dwyer of Little Harbour, Deer Lake; Miss Alma J. Barrett, Lizzie M. Pye, Frances Bungay, M. Canning, Priscilla Humber, Loretta Normore of Corner Brook; and Miss Francis Warren of Humbermouth.[11]

For Ella Powell, the trip wasn't such a big deal. She had already travelled by train from St. John's to Corner Brook, and after living on her own for four years, she was comfortable with solo travel. "I came all by myself," Ella remembered. "I think there were 18 girls on the train and I didn't know any of them. I got on the train in Corner Brook."

Even though Ella was a confident solo traveller, she was still vulnerable. Once the Newfoundland travellers had crossed the Gulf of St. Lawrence and arrived on Cape Breton Island in Nova Scotia, they boarded another train. After the train chugged across Cape Breton, the group, and the train cars, had to board another ferry for a short trip across the Canso Strait from Cape Breton Island to mainland Nova Scotia. That's when Ella found herself in trouble.

A man distracted Ella by showing her a spot on the deck with a special view, and when she returned to her belongings, she discovered that $20 of her travel money had been stolen. Bechtel points out that his mother had only $30, so to have two-thirds of it stolen was a major loss. Ella kept going.

The train transporting the girls and their chaperones eventually made it to Union Station in downtown Toronto. There, they disembarked and boarded a smaller train on a smaller rail line for Hespeler. After a few hours on the smaller train, they arrived at their destination—the Hespeler train station, a few hundred metres past the Dominion Woollens and Worsteds Mill.

The girls, who gathered their trunks and suitcases, were met by more chaperones, who walked them down Queen Street and up the hill to their destinations, the residences of Gordon Hall and Winston Hall.

By the time Eileen's group arrived at Winston Hall, it was late. Her first impression was a lasting one: "The Canadian girls stayed up until 2 a.m. to see them arrive, because they wanted to see the Eskimos from Newfoundland."

Ella

Fortified with a boiled egg and a bowl of Cream of Wheat, Ella drained the last of her cup of tea. She was on the day shift at the mill this week and was due at her post at 8 a.m. Every now and then, early in the morning, Ella thought of her mother's warm homemade bread, spread with butter and molasses, and a pang of homesickness would pass through her body. But Ella had left her family home in Carbonear for jobs in St. John's and Corner Brook several years before she came to Hespeler; so truth be told, she missed bread and molasses less often these days.

Now, she appreciated the rainbow of fresh fruit and vegetables that showed up in regular rotation in the dining room at Winston Hall. Every week, it seemed, there was something she'd never seen before, let alone tasted.

On her way out of the dining room, she spotted a wicker bowl on a table full of round orange fruit. Not oranges—as in the fruit that had shown up in the toe of her Christmas stocking back home—but a lighter orange, slightly fuzzy ball. It took Ella a few seconds to register that these were peaches. Real honest-to-goodness peaches.

Of course, Ella had eaten peaches before, from a tin. In Newfoundland, tinned fruit cocktail was a treat. When Ella had worked at the infirmary in St. John's, fruit cocktail, served in small dishes with a dollop of Bird's Custard, occasionally showed up on the menu. She could see it now, the small squares of pears, peaches, and who knows what else—floating in syrup. She wondered if these peaches would taste the same.

Southwestern Ontario was peach-growing country, and now the peaches were ripe. Farmers sold bushels of peaches at the sides of the roads and in every local market. Fresh peaches in July in Hespeler were as common as wild blueberries on Newfoundland barrens in September. Ella picked a peach from the basket and bit into it.

Her teeth sank through the flesh like a knife cutting through butter. Juice ran down her chin. The flavour exploded in her mouth. Ella felt like she was chewing through a sunny day, one infused with tangy, sweet energy.

Ella flung the peach pit into a nearby wastebasket, used her handkerchief to wipe her face and hands, and then took another peach from the basket to take with her.

She couldn't wait for her mid-morning break.

10

Winston Hall and Gordon Hall

The Newfoundland recruits were about to be immersed in an unfamiliar, noisy, and demanding environment, where the work was tiring and the hours long. More than a paycheque would be needed to convince the new workers to stay. Far from home, the mill girls would need comfort.

The solution? Housing—made especially for "hard working 'nice girls.'"

When young, single women first came to Hespeler in the early 1940s, the company boarded them in private homes. But as the number of mill girls increased, billet families could not keep up. The mill bought a large, two-storey house with wraparound verandahs on both levels, renamed it Gordon Hall, and turned it into a residence for 30 to 50 girls. Other smaller houses around Hespeler accommodated a dozen or so mill girls at a time.

In 1944, a residence built with Canadian government funds opened. Winston Hall housed 165 women. It quickly became a home

Gordon Hall typically housed girls who worked overnight shifts. Courtesy of Hespeler Heritage Centre.

away from home for most of the mill girls and a social hub. Both residences had 24-hour supervision, a house matron, and cooking and housekeeping staff. Winston Hall,

> which houses only girls who are working on textile production with Dominion Woollens, is a real girls' residence. Most of the girls live two in a room, where each has her own comfortable bed, with blonde maple chiffoniers, dressing tables and easy chairs. All the rooms are finished in pastel shades. But they don't have to keep to their rooms, and very few of them do except to write their letters home. There's a very handsome big lounge on the upper floor of

> the two-storey, light gray slate building, complete with chesterfields and deep upholstered chairs and a radio. Off the foyer on the main floor are small sitting rooms where the girls may entertain their friends and relatives.[12]

The April 1944 Dominion Woollens and Worsteds newsletter was equally effusive about the new accommodations:

> It's a good-looking building. The construction is frame, faced with grey asbestos shingles and trimmed in cream. Built on a modified "E" plan, the impressive gothic entrance in the middle wing opens into a comfortable reception lobby. On the one side of the lobby are the administration offices, and on the other side are several "beau parlors" comfortably furnished with chesterfields and easy chairs and designed to give the girl residents at the house a pleasant spot to entertain their friends and families as they would in the privacy of their own homes.
>
> The dining room, at the rear of the entrance lobby, is operated cafeteria style under the supervision of the graduate dietitian, and its staff is trained to provide well-balanced, interesting meals. The dining room doubles as a recreation centre when the tables are pushed back and the ping pong equipment brought

> out. There's a jukebox for dancing, with the proceeds being turned over to the girls' council for recreational purposes.
>
> The second floor of the middle wing is given over largely to an exceedingly comfortable lounge. Walls are done in knotty pine, and the furniture is blonde maple with the many chesterfields in pastel colours. Facing the lounge across the corridor is a sheltered sundeck.[13]

Winston Hall, Gordon Hall, and even private home billets were nothing like the family homes that Daisy, Eileen, Ella, and Dolly had grown up in. The residences were orderly, clean, and stable, with structured rules and regulations. In many cases, for girls who had grown up in crowded homes with a limited diet, the posh accommodations made up for the culture shock of a new country, a new job, and new people.

Daisy, assigned to Gordon Hall, loved it. She enjoyed the camaraderie, food, social activities, and, more than anything, the personal space. "Oh, she thought it was the big city, basically living in the dorms with the other girls," says her daughter.

Gordon Hall was the smaller residence; once Winston Hall opened, Gordon Hall became the home for the young women who worked the overnight shift. Set a short distance from Winston Hall, the Gordon Hall property was lined with trees and shrubs, which absorbed noise from the surrounding streets. Gordon Hall staff scheduled meals and activities around the workers' schedules, with quiet hours from early morning to mid-afternoon so that they could sleep. Breakfast was served until late afternoon and a hot meal at midnight.

The girls from both Winston and Gordon Halls socialized in the lounges and in each other's rooms. Special events—dances and dinners—happened at Winston Hall.

After some time living in Gordon Hall, Daisy, however, missed the rhythms of family life. In particular, she missed living with younger children, so she chose to board with a Hespeler family. But unlike her own home in Nicholsville, the Hespeler family home was more upscale, and Daisy still had her own space. Daisy often showed her daughter the house where she had boarded, which still stands on Queen Street in Hespeler.

"They had the most beautiful home. We called it the castle," remembers Hammond. "[Daisy] had one of the rooms in sort of a turret. She said it was really nice to be there with a family. They had children and she would babysit for them. And she stayed in contact with them all through her life. Their daughter Mary-Lou lives out in Saskatchewan, I believe."

Eileen, who stayed in Winston Hall during her 13 months in Hespeler, was happy living with other girls. "Each room had two girls, and clothes closets and dressing tables and a chest of drawers. There was a common bathroom and shower facilities on each floor," explains her daughter. "There was a dining room and a lounge, no liquor allowed, with a jukebox and a dance floor. She grew up in a big family. I think there was seven of them. So, this was nothing to her to have

Eileen Penney, seated in front, with a group of mill girls during her year in Hespeler.
Courtesy of Terry Gullage.

Eileen Penney, right, holding her skates, with a friend. Courtesy of Terry Gullage.

to share, you know? I never heard her say a bad word about the accommodations or the food or anything else."

Ella was used to living away from home, in workers' accommodations. She had already boarded in several rooms in St. John's and in Corner Brook. But Winston Hall was, by far, the largest and most comfortable. At first, Ella shared a room on the first floor with a girl from Red Bay, Labrador. Later, Ella moved to a larger room on the second floor.

Dominion Woollens and Worsteds even made holidays special so that the girls would not become homesick for their families and want to leave. "Christmas dinner at Winston Hall was always a big deal," Ella recalled. "We always had a big dinner and party at Christmas time at Winston Hall. We had a master of ceremony and we had all the head bosses there for the dinner. They showed us a good time."

The food, which featured prominently in recruitment presentations, met the girls' expectations. There was always plenty of fresh local farm fruit and vegetables and hearty meals to fuel them for long shifts at the mill.

For Newfoundland girls, whose fruit and vegetable experience was limited mainly to wild berries, the occasional apple, and root vegetables, the variety of food was a novelty. Having various meats added to their diets also provided a change from the cod and beef they had been accustomed to at home.

Another novelty for the Newfoundland girls was the luxury of having someone cook and clean for *them*. For the first time, these young women had no responsibilities to their families—no cooking, cleaning, or childminding. When they were not working at the mill, their off-duty hours, for the first time in their lives, were their own.

11

The Mill Floor

The first day of work for the Newfoundland recruits at Dominion Woollens and Worsteds was a day like no other in their lives. They walked down the hill from Winston Hall, across Queen Street and the railway tracks, to the factory buildings and joined hundreds of women, and some men, walking through a gate at the side of one of the buildings, then streaming in the front door to begin their shifts.

A Day in the Life of a Mill Girl, the presentation most of the girls had seen at recruitment meetings, had not prepared them for the reality of a mill shift. From outside, the factory complex looked immense, sprawling as it did along the Speed River; inside, it seemed even bigger.

Most of the Dominion Woollens and Worsteds manufacturing complex was three stories high; some parts, five stories. Inside the buildings was the modern machinery that was designed to turn raw fleece into bolts of cloth, ready to be sewn into Canadian military uniforms or civilian clothes.

Each floor contained large long and wide rooms, with support beams. Double height windows lined each side of the building. Shaded lamps were suspended from the extra high ceilings to illuminate working areas. Massive floor-to-ceiling machines, full of wheels, rollers, cylinders, levers, pulleys, and metal teeth, were lined up across the factory floors. All that industrial technology was powered by a hydroelectric plant on the Speed River.

The working environment was hot, noisy, and dusty, and the factory operated 24 hours a day, Monday to Saturday.

For some of the girls from Newfoundland, who had just travelled several days from home to a different country, this foreign, intense industrial environment was simply too much. Retired mill supervisor Mr. P. Mills recalled one young Newfoundland woman:

> We had one girl come from Newfoundland, [a] young girl. The other girls brought her into my department, she was coming in on the night shift, she got in as far as the dressing room and she would not come out of the dressing room. She burst into tears and she shook and shivered and she just wouldn't. The noise of the big machines, they scared her, the heat, we had to send her back without doing an hour's worth of work. She wasn't the only one but she was a good example. Some of them lasted a few days, but she didn't even come on the floor.[14]

It was a tough environment; even before World War II, the mill had a difficult time keeping workers for more than a few years. A former mill girl, identified by Spring as Mrs. H. Hooper, explained:

> There was no noise control. So the shuttles going on the spinning or the shuttles on the weaving machines, not the shuttles but cones and that the noise of the machinery itself, you had to talk very loud. In some places it was extremely dirty. In the carding room or the dye department it was very dirty. You had to sweep around your own machines.[15]

In all the photos of the young women working in various parts of the factory, no one is wearing earplugs to protect them from loud noise or masks to protect against airborne dust, fibres, or chemicals. Yet, for its time, Dominion Woollens and Worsteds was more safety-minded than most southern Ontario manufacturing facilities.

Hundreds of workers were on shift at any given time. Raw fleece was kept in barns, and then it started its journey in the carding and spinning department. There, workers fed fleece into Garnett machines, a carding machine equipped with rollers, cylinders, and metallic teeth. After carding, the fleece was run through several types of spinning machines, each capable of spinning hundreds of strands of wool at a time. It was a far cry from hand-carding and the foot-operated spinning wheels that women in the mill girls' Newfoundland communities used to make yarn for knitting.

The dyehouse was a separate building because the work was so dangerous. Large quantities of wet and dry wool were fire hazards. Workers dyed the carded wool in metre-high, stainless-steel vats, controlled by the latest technology, automatic timers, and thermostats. Even though the temperatures were controlled, the dyehouse was hotter than the rest of the factory, full of steam from the chemical dye vats. Sometimes one person had to manage several vats at once. Not only was the dyehouse the hottest part of the factory but it smelled the worst from the stench of wet wool and chemicals.

In the weaving room, thousands of strands of this dyed yarn were fed over the workers' heads from machine to machine, as automatic looms transformed the yarn into wide sheets of cloth.

The final cleaning and detailing were done on the cloth in the finishing rooms before it became completed bolts of cloth ready for cutting and sewing.

The machinery was maintained by a team of boiler engineers, plumbers, pipefitters, welders, electricians, and general maintenance staff, almost all men. But during wartime, running the machines became women's work. They loaded the machines with the fleece, wool, and yarn that would be processed to the next stage. When anything went wrong, or became tangled, the women had to unsnarl the mistakes and get the machines operating again. Some workers managed several large industrial machines at once. One mill girl (Mrs. A. Cook) described a typical shift on looms that turned out different sizes of fabric for scarves, hats, pants, skirts, and capes:

> We each had six looms to operate, and if the person beside us happened to be off sick, we had to take half their share. They were heavy machines to operate. It had been just men running the looms before the war. We wove the khaki for the army uniforms. On the looms you were running steady all the time, with three shifts.... You had to be very careful how you tied the knots and worked the knots into the material so that it didn't show.[16]

The machinery was intimidating to most new workers on their first day, whether they were Newfoundlanders or French Canadians from northern Ontario, but the only way to learn the work was to dive in. Each new employee was paired with a more experienced worker, who would train her to use the machine to which she was assigned and show her the routines of the workplace—where to store her belongings, when to take her lunch breaks, and how to sign in and out of her shift.

Eileen's training used this buddy system: "The first job she had, she worked on a machine that made the wool into balls of yarn. She had one day of training, that was it. And then she was promoted shortly to a machine that took the yarn and put it into little spools for the big machines. Afterwards she worked on the one that took the yarn and put it into bobbins and that they used to use on the weaving machine to make the material. This was called cap spinning."

Depending on the machine and department, and depending on the

Workers in the Dominion Woollens and Worsted twisting room, 1943. Photo by Frank Johnston, courtesy of Hespeler Heritage Centre.

knack of the new workers, sometimes only a day of training was needed, sometimes it necessitated several weeks. Once the young women mastered the agility required to operate the machines, the work was straightforward. It was very physical: standing, pushing, pulling, and lifting, or sitting, painstakingly picking at small flaws in finished fabric. Many former mill girls spoke about rewinds and having to redo work on raw material that was running through the machines.

In the drawing and twisting department, workers threaded the strands through clattering floor-to-ceiling machines that twisted strands of wool together to form yarn, each machine twisting hundreds of strands at a time, with dozens of machines lined up and down the factory floor. As Ella described it,

> [We worked] the wool machines, making the yarn smaller. There was all kinds of machines. You'd hang the bobbins up on a machine and they'd unroll on smaller bobbins and be smaller each time. We had to weigh them—a certain amount of pounds would go in fours, because the fours would go into one on the front of the machine. Hang them up on the back of the machine and take the small bobbins off when they were filled at the front.

Despite the intricate, large machinery and inexperienced staff, there were few accidents. Most of the incidents recalled by some of the mill girls happened to men, who lost a finger, or even a hand. Once the young women became familiar with the machines, the tasks were repetitive; the safety challenge was making sure that they paid attention to what they were doing.

After spinning, the material was transformed into large bolts of woven, worsted wool cloth. Then, in the finishing rooms, more workers did more tedious tasks, as described by Mrs. Laundry: "I started ironing selvages on the cloth [that's] the seam that turned over, you iron that out so that it wouldn't get cut going through the shears. Then I did a little specking after that. Specking is picking the little white specks out of the cloth."[17]

One male supervisor noted that the young women often came to their first day of work wearing dresses, but they soon changed into coveralls and headscarves as they adapted to the work.

An unidentified worker in the spinning room at Dominion Woollens and Worsteds, 1942. Photo by Frank Johnston, courtesy of Hespeler Heritage Centre.

During the 1940s, for six days a week, 24 hours a day, hundreds of workers, mostly women, piled in and out of the factory for 10-hour shifts. That was their war effort—on the front lines of the supply chain. In the second half of the 1940s, they were on the advance team for Canada's postwar economic growth and prosperity. Hardly anyone noticed that much of this home-front army consisted of teenagers and young women from the foreign, and mostly frozen or foggy, country of Newfoundland.

12

Dolly on the Job

Work at the mill was hard and the hours long, but Dolly took to work at Dominion Woollens and Worsteds and life at Winston Hall like a fish to water—the fresh water of the Speed River instead of the salt water of St. John's harbour.

"I think her attitude was, 'Work me like a dog, but I'm on my own,'" says her daughter. At the mill, Dolly was first assigned to the spinning room. It was tricky work, carefully feeding thread onto multiple rapidly spinning automatic bobbins. Tangles were frequent, and she needed a quick hand and eye to keep everything spinning smoothly. Used to juggling housework, children, a job at the Newfoundland Hotel, and the general chaos of life at home, Dolly was a natural.

Dolly was so good at her job that mill photographers documented her work on the factory floor, and her smiling face was used in recruitment photos and presentations. Once her skill in the spinning department was proven, Dolly was moved to other jobs in other rooms. She became familiar with all stages of producing bolts of khaki-coloured woollen cloth.

As far as Dolly was concerned, this was an upgrade from her life on the Outer Battery. She instantly loved Winston Hall. She shared her room with only one person, a young woman her own age. And, for the first time in her life, she had her own bed.

The dormitory-style bathrooms were a revelation as well. Dolly had lived in a house with many younger brothers and sisters and no running water. Now she had access to a row of cubicles with flush toilets and a row of sinks with taps that, when you turned them, water, cold and hot, simply flowed out. Dolly could stand at a sink and brush her teeth uninterruptedly.

The food that had been shown in the recruitment slide shows lived up to Dolly's expectations and beyond. At home, Dolly had access to fresh fruit—other than berries picked on nearby Signal Hill—only at Christmas. Now, every day, there was a selection of fruit, grown at local farms in the area. Fresh apples, peaches, cherries.

Life at Winston Hall came with another feature that Dolly had never encountered—regular visits to a doctor. The only time Dolly's family, or most families in her neighbourhood, had seen a doctor was when someone was seriously ill. The girls at Winston Hall could book routine doctor visits, which, for Dolly, was the one thing she could not take in stride. On her first visit to a doctor's office, the male doctor tried to give her a full examination, which included a gynecological exam. According to her daughter, "Mom just lost her nut and went screaming from the room." Eventually, Dolly calmed down, and visits to the doctor, dentist, and optometrist became part of her routine, a routine that was unheard of in her Newfoundland life.

Dolly worked long shifts, up to 12 hours at a time, six days a week. The work was hot, loud, and demanding. But, compared to living at home, where every waking minute was spent helping someone else in the Walsh family, Dolly had time to herself, independence, and money in her pocket.

Other Newfoundland mill girls recounted similar stories. Daisy never talked much about her actual work at the mill, but her daughter remembers her mother always being ready for hard, physical work, from shovelling snow to taking on occasional shift work at factories when Hammond was young. Bechtel's mother, Ella, told him about the fun that she had had with her friends at Winston Hall in her spare time. According to Gullage, Eileen, too, remembered her time at the mill as being more about the adventure of living away from home and helping out with the war effort than about the hard, overnight hours on the mill floor.

Eileen

Eileen looked at her weekly pay stub. After deductions, she had $9.39, all to herself. She had worked hard all week on the overnight shift and now it was time to treat herself.

She set her alarm to get up earlier on Friday afternoon, to walk down Queen Street to the Toronto Dominion Bank, where she'd set up a bank account. There, she could deposit some of her paycheque and take the rest in cash. Even though she had to report to work at 11 p.m. that night, she could still go to the dance at Winston Hall for a few hours before punching in for her shift. After a week of having her hair tied up in a kerchief on the dusty mill floor, she wanted to show up at the dance looking her best. She wanted the professionals to set her hair in curls.

Eileen had a 3:30 p.m. appointment at the Beauty Crest Beauty Parlour, but she still had half an hour to wait. Enough time for a browse at Prong's Books. She could pick up a romance novel and a few magazines to take to the beach at Puslinch Lake on Sunday.

She would miss the early mealtime at the residence while she was getting her hair done, but she would order a grilled cheese sandwich at the snack bar before strolling back to the residence to start her day: first, a dance, and, then, a work shift.

This all felt a little like having dessert before the main course, and briefly, Eileen felt a pang of guilt. Then again, she thought, she was here, in Hespeler, working at Dominion Woollens and Worsteds to contribute to the war effort. Getting her hair done and buying treats was all part of supporting the troops.

13

Payday

The mill girls were doing the work of men at Dominion Woollens and Worsteds but they were not being paid the same as the men who had done the work. The company may have been progressive in hiring women and in its recruitment and retention strategies, but it drew the line at pay equity. On average, women were paid about 48 cents an hour; men doing the same work, 60 cents. Spring's research suggests that the Canadian government assumed that women would only be temporarily in the workforce during the war, and when the men returned, they would return home.

Eileen saved her pay stubs. Her wages were 49 cents an hour—the night shifts paid more than the days, so she chose to work nights. She often worked 10-hour shifts. A 46-hour workweek brought in $23.38, $9.39 after deductions. "In the meantime there was a victory bond that she was paying $4 into every paycheck," Gullage adds. "And then the 'sundry' was $7. I'm wondering if sundry meant what you had to pay for your room and board."

Ella also saved her pay stubs. On one of them, for 40 hours of work, before deductions, she was paid $33.90. After deductions, including income tax, sick benefits, and union dues, she received $11.14. Other deductions: $8 for sundries and $10 for the Christmas fund.

"They had to pay for their room and board and they also had to make a contribution to their travel expenses to get them there," Spring qualifies. "I don't think they paid the full amount, but they did make a contribution with each paycheck towards their fare. So they never really started to make more money until after about a year. And then they still had their living expenses."

Yet the money at the mill was better than they could have earned at other jobs in the area, and compared with the money they could have made in Newfoundland, they were doing well. Little mention was made of sending money home to their families. For the families of Ella, Eileen, Daisy, and Dolly, having one fewer mouth to feed and person to clothe was enough. Hespeler also changed with the influx of mill girls. It benefitted financially from the company's decision to recruit these women. Their interest in fashion meant that local clothing merchants, anxious to encourage the women to spend money in their stores, catered to current fashion trends. Three dress shops—Helen's, Adler's, and Collins—were especially popular.

Dolly's daughter remembers her mother telling her that one of the first things she did after she became a mill girl was make a dental appointment. Dolly wasn't the only young woman from Newfoundland who had never seen a dentist. Turner spoke with several former mill girls who had spent their first paycheques catching up on their health care and booking appointments with dentists and optometrists on Queen Street in Hespeler. After their teeth and eyes had been taken care of, they spent their money on more fanciful things.

"A lot of them came into the community and they patronized the clothing stores with the money they made working at the mill," Turner points out. "They bought new clothes, they bought new shoes, they had their hair done, they went to the salons. They put a lot of the money back into the community."

The mill girls also patronized clothing boutiques in nearby Preston and Galt, which could be reached via electric streetcar or special charter buses and always had appealing new fashions. Shops catering to hair, makeup, and magazines, all of which were considered luxuries at home in Newfoundland, targeted teenagers and women in their early 20s.

Photos of dances and formal events attended by mill girls show fashionable dresses, hair, and makeup. Outdoor photos show the girls modelling new, fashionable winter coats. The girls always accessorized their clothing with bright lipstick and well-tended curls.

The children of Dolly, Daisy, Eileen, and Ella spoke of their mothers' love of fashion, how well dressed and coiffed they were, whether they were taking care of the children at home or going to a fancy party. If the girls sent money home to their families, or built a small nest egg of savings for themselves, they didn't talk about it.

Eileen's income at the mill during the war was comparable to the money that her future husband, Gordon, made at the Corner Brook pulp and paper mill after the war. "I would imagine that it [Eileen's pay] wasn't too bad, because I saw another wage slip for my father from the mill [in Corner Brook] when he first started. There wasn't a very big amount of money. He was earning, like, $20 a week or something like that," Gullage remembers.

14

The Official Activities

The "hard working 'nice girls'" recruited by Dominion Woollens and Worsteds did work hard. They punched in for 10- or 12-hour shifts, day or night, and had only Sunday off each week. On Sunday morning, most of the mill girls went to church, walking together in small groups to the nearby Presbyterian, Anglican, Roman Catholic, and Baptist churches.

But they were young and had lots of energy, and when they were not on the job, they did not have to cook, clean, or care for their younger siblings or answer to their parents. They also had money in their pockets. They could go out and have fun. They were free, but not so free that they could do whatever they wanted.

Turner describes Dominion Woollens and Worsteds as a "paternalistic employer." The company made sure that each family in Hespeler had a member working at the mill during the Great Depression. In the 1940s, when the mill began recruiting hundreds of young single women and girls, away from the constraints of their families, the company had a vested interest in making sure that these girls would continue to report to work and not leave due to homesickness, boredom when not working, or, the biggest worry of all, unplanned pregnancies.

"The mill really tried to keep them entertained," Spring explains. "It was a smart move economically, because if you have happy workers, they're going to continue to work there."

Dominion Woollens and Worsteds put a considerable amount of time, money, and staffing, into keeping the young women busy at wholesome activities. Daisy took part in many of them. "My mom has told me that there were dances that they attended," says her daughter. "She played hockey. She was on the Dominion Woollens baseball team. They had trips into Toronto and bus tours to different places."

The mill girls loved music of the popular swing orchestras of the 1940s and they loved to dance. The Winston Hall dining hall could be converted into a recreation room with a dance floor, and it had a jukebox on which the girls could play the latest hits. Dances were so popular that the company's Recreation Club organized them at the local Oddfellows Hall, hiring local dance orchestras. Because many young men in Hespeler served overseas, the company invited young men from the Galt Aircraft School and the Galt naval training program to provide dance partners for the mill girls. These events, and the invitation for young single men to meet young single women, created a stir in Hespeler. The company worked with the town's police to make sure that the dances didn't get too rowdy. When those dances did get out of hand, the company looked for other ways to let the mill girls burn off their youthful energy.

Scenes from a dance at the Oddfellows Hall.
Photos by F.C. Hutchings.

The Dominion Woollens and Worsted Recreation club worked with the mill girls to develop a range of activities for the workers on different shifts. The night workers had a Wednesday afternoon bowling league at a bowling alley in nearby Preston. Here is the newsletter's account of a social for the day-shift workers:

> On Saturday, Feb. 12th, over 300 employees turned up at the card party and dance, organized by the Recreation Club for the day shift, in the Oddfellows' Hall. Some fifty aircraftmen from the Galt Aircraft School were in attendance. During the early part of the evening euchre was in play, prize for high score going to Fred Humphreys, consolation prize to Jim Ball, and Mrs. John Mclaughlin was awarded the prize for lone hands. Following the card game, dancing got underway. Highlights of the evening's dancing were the "Conga line," and a square dance—no hillbillies—but how they could square it off! The evening wound up with refreshments and a sing song. To the Recreation Club committee and the girls who prepared the refreshments goes all the credit for a successful party. This was the first in a series of parties which the recreation Club is planning to organize.[18]

As the 1940s progressed, and more and more young women arrived in Hespeler to work at the mill, the company newsletter reported on new activities. Several softball teams were formed, with one team travelling extensively to play in tournaments. There was a tennis court and plans for a horseshoe pitch at the residences. In the winter, the company built an outdoor skating rink.

By 1945, a musical society had formed, and the mill supported an orchestra and a choir, made up of mill workers, with a well-paid musical conductor. Both groups held regular concerts around Hespeler, usually at St. Andrew's Presbyterian Church, the largest church in Hespeler.

Excursions were also popular. The mill's buses took the girls shopping in Preston or to the beach at Puslinch Lake. Several special trips were organized each year. The mill chartered buses to take the workers on daylong excursions to Niagara Falls and the Canadian National Exhibition in Toronto, both eye-opening experiences for young women from rural Newfoundland and rural northern Ontario.

The company's major event every year was one not only for the mill workers but also for everyone in Hespeler—the annual mill picnic:

> The picnic of August 9, 1946 was one to remember. It was the first mill picnic since the end of the second world war. The mill whistle sounded at 6 a.m., to let the townspeople know it was time to gather at the train station. Mill girls, mill bosses, and families with young children boarded a train, 18 cars long, to the strains of the town band. Merchants in Hespeler closed their shops for the day and came along, too.

> The train pulled away from the station, stopped to pick up more mill workers and their families at Beaverdale, Preston, and Galt, then headed for Hamilton, and the ferry at Lake Ontario to take everyone—1,200 people in all—to the beach at Port Dalhousie for the day. There were games—plant workers versus managers and town leaders, midway rides for the children, a picnic meal, countless softball games—all on the company's dime. Young workers danced on the decks of the return ferry. The train, full of tired but happy revelers, pulled back into the station in Hespeler after midnight. The whole event was covered extensively by the DW&W newsletter, which declared it the best picnic ever, and "here's to a bigger and better one next year!"[19]

During Christmas, the mill closed for three days, but the girls from Newfoundland and northern Ontario were too far from home to visit their families for the holidays. The staff at the mill residences were aware that the young girls experienced bouts of homesickness. At Christmas, Winston and Gordon Halls were lavishly decorated, complete with Christmas trees, and the girls were served a festive Christmas dinner. Santa Claus visited the residences with gifts for everyone. The Christmas fund deduction from the girls' paycheques was put to good use.

15

The *DW&W News*

"We know absolutely nothing about publishing a newspaper," announced the editors of the first edition of the Dominion Woollens and Worsteds monthly newsletter in July 1941. "That will make it more interesting than most papers."[20]

Dominion Woollens and Worsteds went further than other large manufacturing companies in supporting the Canadian war effort. In addition to urging its workers to buy Victory Bonds, the company started the *DW&W News* as a morale booster for its workers who served overseas in the military; it was a way to keep them connected with their workplace and in their community.

It soon became clear that the overseas soldiers weren't reading the newsletter to learn about new stainless steel dye vats installed at the mill or the quality of wool fleece from Australia or South Africa.

The first editions were black and white, with front-page stories on mill news and a photo and short profile of a male mill worker serving in active duty overseas. On page 2 was what these men were

Page 2 of the *DW&W News* for July 1951. Daisy Nichols poses in her swimsuit in the lower left photo. Courtesy of City of Cambridge Archives.

looking for: five smiling young women, in glamorous one-piece swimsuits and new sandals, posing arm in arm on the beach at nearby Puslinch Lake—with the cheeky caption "No assignment too arduous for our photographer."

"Publishing this newsletter required a fair bit of human resources to get done. And it was a really popular newsletter. And so the girls were quite proud if they had been part of this newsletter," Spring comments.

The four-page *DW&W News* was printed on glossy paper stock, with almost every story accompanied by a photo. These stories were a mix of textile industry news, developments at the mill, updates on mill workers serving overseas, social and community events, and breathless updates on the lives of the mill girls.

On the inside pages of the newsletter were photos of the young female mill workers on the job—working different pieces of machinery or in a group photo with their coworkers. Their lives outside the factory were also closely documented in articles and announcements about the various activities that the mill arranged for off-duty workers. Those articles included photos of the mill girls at leisure—in a softball team, bowling, or taking part in a concert with the mill orchestra and choir. As the newsletter grew in popularity, more glamour photos of the young women, often in swimsuits, were included.

The January 1947 edition of the *DW&W News* devoted an entire page to thumbnail sketches of several young mill women. The newsletter had a few paragraphs about Maude Whelan of St. John's, noting that her father was a disabled World War I veteran and that she had an interest in drama: "Maude took up residence in Winston Hall on her arrival in Hespeler and it has been a 'home away from home' ever since. Maude told us she likes Canada better than Newfoundland, but failed to tell us why. Of course, we have our own suspicions."

Mary Brennan, the newsletter noted, was from Placentia, near where the historic Atlantic Charter was drafted, after a top-secret meeting between British prime minister Winston Churchill and American president Franklin Roosevelt in 1941: "Mary is an experienced twister operator, but in her leisure moments finds time to express her musical ability as a pianist as well as to work on her hobby of collecting pictures of movie stars of which she has an interesting collection. Like Maude Whelan, Mary says she likes Canada very much, finding many more interesting things to do than in Newfoundland."

The newsletter quickly became more than a monthly update for overseas young men (mostly) serving in Europe in the war—it was a modern look at young women living their best lives in Hespeler.

DW&W News was read by mill employees and most citizens of Hespeler—as almost every household had someone working at the mill—and it was also taken on the road by recruiters to show to those young women they hoped to hire.

According to Stapleton, the newsletter made an impact in Newfoundland: "I can only imagine being a 16-year-old girl with few prospects at the time. In comes someone who says, well, here is where you're going to live and we're going to give you all this food and you're going to be taking glamour shots and you're going to be part of this amazing war effort to buck up the boys."

After World War II, the newsletter evolved and grew in popularity. Puslinch Lake, a nearby beach and boating area, became prominent in the *DW&W News*. Not that it had anything to do with the textile industry. It was a scenic spot to get photos of the mill girls in their swimsuits.

By the late 1940s, newsletter front pages looked more like the covers of a women's fashion magazine. The title was in a colour banner across the top of the page. The front-page mill girl was posed in a glamour shot on a beach or in a studio. The photos were so popular that the newsletter profiled photographer Frank Johnston, who also worked at the mill's testing lab. The May 1948 edition of the newsletter shows him at work in a studio, getting ready to shoot photos of a mill girl posed teasingly in a boudoir-like setting.

That boudoir-like setting. Photographs of employees in their swimsuits. Photo captions with double entendres. The mill girls were objectified and exploited for their looks. No corporate human resources department would let a company newsletter or social media accounts publish material like that in 2025. But there are no records or anecdotes of complaints about the newsletter. On the contrary, being featured in the newsletter was a thrill.

"I just loved it [the newsletter] because these were young women who were in their prime," Spring states. "Oftentimes you could see even with age, what beautiful people they were. The photographer really captured their youth and their beauty."

Daisy appeared in the July 1951 issue on page 2, which was entirely taken up by three photos—vibrant young women who

DW&W NEWS

Published for the Hespeler, Ontario, Plant of Dominion Woollens and Worsteds, Limited

Vol. VI JANUARY - 1947 No. 7

Thumbnail Sketching » »

When the Company purchased Winston Hall from Wartime Housing Limited early in December, the local newspapers wanted something for their news columns. After we had given them everything we could think of, however, there still wasn't enough to compete against an average-sized want ad. It was then that we realized that the most interesting feature of Winston Hall is the people who live there.

Accordingly, it was felt that the best way for the News to cover the Winston Hall purchase is to publish thumbnail sketches of a few of the girls who have lived there the longest. Here they are:

* * * *

MAUDE WHALEN

When the Company's representative, Russell Wehner, went to Newfoundland in 1944 with an interesting offer to Newfoundland girls who were willing to come to Canada (Hespeler in particular) to help produce khaki cloth for our soldiers, Maude Whalen lost no time in signing up with D. W. & W. Maude knew of the ravages of war first hand since her father was permanently disabled while on active service in World War I.

Born in St. John's, Newfoundland, she lived in that city until she left for Canada. Maude took up residence in Winston Hall on arrival in Hespeler and to her it has been a 'home away from home' ever since. Maude told us she likes Canada better than Newfoundland, but failed to tell us why. Of course we have our own suspicions.

Maude told this writer that for some time she has been interested in dramatics, and during her school years portrayed many parts in various school plays. We mention this, hoping that those in the Recreation Club who may be looking for talent to form a "Dramatic Club" may take the tip.

* * * *

MARY BRENNAN

Mary Brennan made her first trip to Canada in 1944. She adopted Hespeler as her home town and Winston Hall as her home and she has lived there ever since.

Mary was born in the small town of Placentia, Newfoundland. Hearing the name Placentia, we were reminded that it was off the shores of this ancient town in Placentia Bay that the Atlantic Charter, one of the most remarkable documents ever drafted, grew out of the historic meeting in 1941 between Winston Churchill and the late President Roosevelt. Mary is an experienced twister operator, but in her leisure moments finds time to express her musical ability as a pianist as well as to work at her hobby of collecting pictures of movie stars of which she has an interesting collection.

Like Maude Whalen, Mary says she likes Canada very much, finding many more interesting things to do than in Newfoundland.

* * * *

MARY DWYER

Mary Dwyer was another of the Newfoundland girls to brave the submarine infested waters of the Gulf of St. Lawrence during the height of the war in 1944 to assist D. W. & W. spin and twist the many thousands of pounds of worsted yarn required to keep the yardage of khaki uniform cloth flowing out of Hespeler Mill to our boys overseas.

On arrival in Hespeler, Mary checked in at Winston Hall which she now regards as her permanent Hespeler residence. Mary comes from a large family (six sisters and two brothers) whose home is in Deer Lake, Newfoundland. We find Mary is an experienced traveller having come to Canada on a previous occasion when she spent fourteen months as a waitress in Sydney, Nova Scotia. While not certain that she will remain in Canada permanently, Mary is enjoying her stay in Hespeler. The Canadian winter especially appeals to her, as she is very fond of winter sports . . . skiing in particular.

* * * *

EDITH WHITE

Edith White of Schumacker is one of the many northern Ontario girls on the Company's staff. Deciding to leave the rugged north with its glittering gold in the capable hands of her father who is employed at Hallnor Mines, and others, who like him, are skilled miners, Edith came south early in the spring of 1944. Winston Hall was scarcely ready for occupation when she arrived in Hespeler, but the doors being open, Edith slipped in, signed the register and since then has been one of its regular residents.

Edith is one of the experienced Comb operators whose responsibility it is to see that the combing operation is exact and complete, as combing to a large extent controls the quality of wool tops which guarantees the spinning of a strong, elastic and even yarn.

During her leisure time, Edith may be often seen with her camera, collecting additional evidence to prove the interest photography holds for her.

* * * *

CLARICE DONNAIT

Another Dominion Woollens girl from the north is Clarice Donnait. Clarice was born at Field which is near North Bay. Leaving three brothers and four sisters at home, Clarice struck out for herself and has made her home in Hespeler for the past two and one-half years. Shortly after Winston Hall had been officially opened Clarice moved in. She liked the congenial comradeship among the girls so gave out her mailing address 'c/o Winston Hall'. Her mail continues to come addressed that way. During the war years Clarice was a machine operator in the Worsted Card Room, but is now an experienced operator in the Combing Department. Last summer Clarice's sister Marie started to work

Continued on page four

Winston Hall Cafeteria

Courtesy of City of Cambridge Archives.

worked at the mill. The top two young women pose on a tennis court with two handsome young men, all holding tennis rackets. In the lower right, two girls look up from the bow of a small wooden boat, ready for an adventure. Daisy, in the bottom left, perches on a rock at the water's edge, in a wet, form-fitting one-piece swimsuit, her hair in perfect pin curls, and smiling coquettishly at the camera.

The newsletters were prized keepsakes because the girls were featured in it. But it's unlikely that Daisy, or any other of the Newfoundland bathing beauties, would have sent home copies of the newsletter to their parents. It had been difficult enough to get permission from their families to leave; the last thing their parents would want to find out was that their daughters were posing in swimsuit photo features.

Yet, Daisy was proud enough of her photo that her daughter still has a copy, who enjoys how the newsletter featured her mother and the other mill girls, even some of the outlandish scenarios that Frank Johnston dreamed up for a cover photo. One photo, taken at an airport in Kitchener, had two young mill girls seated in the cockpit of a two-seater airplane. "And [Frank] superimposed it onto an aerial view of the mill," says Spring. "So, it looks like these two women are in a plane flying over the mill."

The young women had watched the recruiting presentation *A Day in the Life of a Mill Girl* and been sold the idea that working at Dominion Woollens and Worsteds would be like starring in the most exciting film version of their own young lives.

The *DW&W News* became their version of a Hollywood magazine.

Dolly

Dolly and her friends loved music and dancing, and the time and place for that was Friday night at Glick's Dance Hall. Glick's wasn't glitzy, but it was a large hall on the second floor of the Glick Building on Queen Street, above a row of shops. Once the shops closed for the evening, the second floor hopped. And this particular Friday night was especially hopping.

Production at the mill that week was in overdrive, and most of the girls had worked extra hours. But it was Friday night and payday; Dolly and her mill friends were ready to let off steam.

Dolly and the rest of the girls danced not only with boys from Hespeler but from Hamilton, Brantford, and Kitchener. Although the dance hall did not serve alcohol, beer and whiskey had been flowing—from the bar in the Queen Hotel across the street and from flasks that both the girls and the boys hurriedly drank outside.

The musicians were local Hespeler players, and they knew all the hits from the big bands—Guy Lombardo and his Royal Canadians, the Glenn Miller Orchestra, Benny Goodman and his Big Band. The floorboards shuddered as the crowd danced to "Take the 'A' Train," "Pennsylvania 6-5000," and "Chattanooga Choo Choo." When the band slowed down to play "Always," Dolly noticed that something was up with her friend, Olive.

Olive had been dancing most of the night with a young, curly-haired blond fellow named Herbert from Kitchener. But her former beau, John, from the air base in Galt, had been leaning against the wall for the past 10 minutes or so, shooting increasingly hostile looks toward Olive and Herbert and taking surreptitious swigs from a flask in his coat pocket.

Suddenly, John strode to the dance floor, shoved Herbert aside, and began dancing with Olive. Dolly, who had been taking a break at a nearby table, rushed to Olive's side. By then, Herbert had thrown a punch at John. John swung back. Dancers backed away from the men. Before more punches could be thrown, Big Cuno, the tall, blocky dance hall bouncer, left his spot by the door and waded into the dance floor fight. He expertly grabbed both John and Herbert by their shirt collars and dragged them toward the exit. With a final shove from Big Cuno, John and Herbert were out the door, at the top of a steep flight of stairs. Both young men tumbled down the steps, landing in a heap at the bottom.

Dolly and Olive rushed down the stairs after them. The quartet were now outside on Main Street. John had a nosebleed, Herbert a split lip and blood dripping from a cut on his forehead, thanks to smacking his head on the bottom step.

John and Herbert looked at each other. Dolly and Olive watched. The two men shook hands, turned, and walked in opposite directions down the street. Upstairs, the band finished playing "Always" to a smattering of applause.

"They don't call this place 'The Bucket of Blood' for nothing," commented Dolly.

"I suppose we should go back up?"

"Of course!"

16

The Bucket of Blood

The mill girls loved to dance. They danced to records on the jukebox at the residence lounge at Winston Hall; they loved the dances put on by the staff at Winston Hall and at the local legion. They even travelled to dances at the military base in Galt.

But when they wanted to cut loose, they headed to dance halls that had no affiliation with Dominion Woollens and Worsteds. Nearly every town in the area—Galt, Preston, Kitchener, and Guelph—had a dance hall. The most popular one for the mill girls, which they called the Bucket of Blood, was just a few minutes down Queen Street, in downtown Hespeler.

The Bucket of Blood, aka Glick's Dance Hall, was located on the second floor of the Glick Building, a two-storey business complex built in 1877. On the first floor were several shops, including a jewelry store. The second floor was taken up entirely by the dance hall.

The entrance to Glick's Dance Hall was a door on the right side of the building. Patrons climbed a narrow, steep set of stairs, wide enough to allow two people to squeeze abreast. At the top of the stairs was the entrance to the dance hall; but first, entry had to be approved by the hall's legendary bouncer.

Big Cuno Possobon, an imposing man of Italian heritage, sat at the top of the stairs.

"He looked you over well," Turner explains. Big Cuno looked for signs of trouble—signs that the mill girls and their beaus might be drunk, and signs that someone might be sneaking in alcohol, because Glick's Dance Hall, like most of the dance halls in the neighbouring towns, was a dry venue.

The mill girls always found a way around dance hall rules. As they and their friends would have a few drinks before going to the bar, they arrived primed and ready to dance. Some of them would sneak in flasks in their pockets.

Other times, they walked down the steep stairs and back onto Queen Street to get "fresh air," which, for them, meant the indoor air across the street at the Queen Hotel's bar to quench their thirst. Then they went back across the street, up the steep stairs, appearing sober enough to the watchful and suspicious eyes of Big Cuno, and onto the dance floor.

When the dance hall was full and the band was hopping, so were the dancers. They made the light fixtures in the first-floor shops rattle. Glick's Dance Hall was a volatile cocktail of live music, alcohol, hormones, young women cutting loose after a week of hard work, and young men cutting loose from their structured life on the nearby military base. Anything could happen, and it often did.

When fights were about to break out, Big Cuno was ready to take control of the situation and eject the offenders.

"If Cuno caught them, he would just throw them down the stairs," Turner adds.

Those steep, narrow stairs with no landing, made for a rough fall. Anyone who was kicked out of Glick's Dance Hall never forgot it. If the dancers were already fighting, maybe the blood was already flowing. A drunken tumble down Glick's stairs guaranteed extra cuts, and definitely bruises. Outside Glick's, the fight often continued; other times, the fall knocked the fight out of the young men, and occasionally, the young women.

Daisy

Eight of them were crammed into the twin room. Joan and Hilda were perched in front of the dresser mirror, setting each other's hair in curlers and wondering which boys from the air base would be at the Winston Hall dance on Saturday night. Mary and Bernice were stretched out on the twin beds, trading fashion magazines, earmarking the pages of dresses they liked and debating whether the styles would be available at the dress boutique in Preston. On the floor, a fast and furious game of cards was going on, with four players, sitting with their backs against the beds.

Daisy and Vera used to play 120s back home in Nicholsville and Badger, and after a few months at Winston Hall, they had taught most of the girls on their floor the popular Newfoundland card game. Iris from North Bay, Ontario, took to 120s like a fish to water, and Peter, their regular second-floor visitor, was hooked on the game as well. Peter and Iris were formidable opponents to Daisy and Vera.

When the clock down the hall chimed, signalling the top of the hour, Peter was studying his hand, deciding whether to bid or pass. A few seconds passed. The group heard the distant sound of footsteps and then a key rattling. The matron was doing her room check. It was lights-out time. All the mill girls were to be in their own rooms, and no visitors were allowed.

Peter's eyes widened over his hand of cards.

Winston Hall was an all-girls residence, and the second floor was strictly off-limits to all male visitors. In theory, Peter should have gotten no farther into Winston Hall than the small sitting rooms off the main foyer downstairs. That's where the mill girls were supposed to entertain their relatives and friends.

But, where there were rules, and more than 100 scrappy, small-town girls living under one roof, there were ways to get around them. All Peter had to do was climb up the trellis on the side of the building, tap on the window at the end of the second-floor hall, and one of the girls would raise the sash and let him in. Later, Peter would let himself out the same way. He was an honorary second-floor Winston Hall resident, as far as the girls were concerned.

The friends scrambled into action. Magazines and hair rollers were dropped, as the girls scattered to their rooms. Daisy had the longest sprint, to her room at the end of the hall, by Peter's exit window. But tonight, Peter had left it too late. The matron was already at the opposite end of the hallway. Peter would never get that exit window open without being caught. Daisy yanked Peter into her room.

"Under here!" Daisy hissed. Peter took a deep breath and slid underneath Daisy's bed. The mattress sank a few inches as Daisy leapt into bed, ready for room check.

"Lights out, Daisy," said the matron.

"Yes, ma'am. Goodnight," responded Daisy sweetly.

Peter was trying not to sneeze out the dust bunnies under the bed.

The matron had finished checking the rooms on one side of the hallway. Now she had to go down the other side of the hall. Daisy listened carefully as the footsteps grew fainter. She peeked out. The coast was clear.

"Peter, go NOW!" Daisy hissed.

Peter slid out from under the bed, out the door, and through the window in less time than it would take Daisy to deal out a hand of cards.

17

Mill Girls Wild and Free

The managers at Dominion Woollens and Worsteds knew that the less time the mill girls spent at the Bucket of Blood, the better it was for business. The company needed its workers to be happy, healthy, and ready to work. It made sure that the girls had activities to occupy their non-working hours, and the *DW&W News* enthusiastically documented their participation in these company-sponsored activities. And if that wasn't enough to discourage shenanigans, Winston and Gordon Halls had curfews and house matrons to monitor the girls.

But a group of teenagers and young women, away from their families and their families' expectations, always found a way to engage in unsanctioned adventures.

"This was before the 1960s." Turner refers to an era in which attitudes toward what young people could do were a little more lax. "You had young girls with money in their pockets, and no supervision."

Nicholson puts it more bluntly: "Winston Hall had a great little reputation. It was like Frosh Week at a university." Dolly had recounted ways the mill girls outsmarted their matrons: Winston Hall girls would sign in with their matron before their 11 p.m. curfew and then use the windows of their residence rooms to come and go or to smuggle boys in and out. For the girls who were most inclined to want after-hours adventures, main-floor residence rooms were preferable. According to Nicholson, "They would sneak out and party until the cows came home, then come back, wash, change, and go to work."

Gordon Hall was different—it was set up for the young women who worked night shifts. The staff at Gordon Hall ran it on night-shift hours—the building was quiet until about 4 p.m. to allow the workers to sleep. The meals reflected their working hours: a late afternoon breakfast and a hot meal at midnight. Because of Gordon Hall's unusual schedule and extended quiet hours, it was trickier to get up to mischief there. When the Gordon Hall girls wanted off-the-books fun, they hung out at the lounges in Winston Hall, where getaway plans were whispered among groups.

Nicholson and Hammond have gathered snippets of conversations from their mothers, Dolly and Daisy, about what they did. Dolly and her friends Olive and Irene loved going to dance halls, both in Hespeler and in nearby towns. It was easy for them to get to dance halls in Preston and Galt on the electric trolley that ran from downtown Hespeler to the downtowns of the two neighbouring towns, right where the action was.

"Someone might have a mickey. The girls would be pretty lit and having fun," Nicholson explains.

The mill girls enjoyed themselves and partied in a way that they couldn't if they had been living with their families. Many experimented with alcohol. Even at official mill social activities, they often smuggled flasks of rum and whiskey to liven up their atmosphere.

This did not go unnoticed by the young men in the area. "There are stories of young men coming in from Brantford and from Hamilton and from Kitchener-Waterloo and Guelph, coming down to Hespeler in the hopes of meeting one of these young girls. It was like flies to honey," claims Turner.

Boys all over southwestern Ontario knew that, in Hespeler, there were buildings full of single girls away from their families. Some of them hung around the mill parking lot hoping to talk to the girls as they left the building at the end of their shifts. Other boys skipped the mill and headed to Winston Hall.

At one point, a security guard was hired to watch the outside of the residences and prevent boys from crawling in through the windows. As some of the boys that hung around the residence knew that the security guard liked to drink, they brought him alcohol. Once he was drinking, or drunk, the boys simply walked around to the back door and the girls let them in.

Hespeler females who were still living at home with their parents and siblings were also well aware of the mill girls' activities. As Turner relates, "They looked upon the mill girls that were coming in as competition for the last remaining young men in the community, because most of them were off to war and they [local girls] saw them as rivals. So there was some animosity towards them. There's even been some talk about fights going on between local girls and the mill girls over a particular eligible young gentleman. The jealousy didn't run deep, but it was there."

Both the mill and local girls remembered this dynamic for decades. The former mill girls that Spring talked to in the 1980s remembered the competition for boyfriends between mill and local girls. In addition to being unsupervised, the mill girls had enough money to pay for local boys' gasoline and for the drinks and other expenses of a night out. As Mrs. J. Doyle told Spring:

> The girls themselves just ran wild. A lot of them were from tiny little places smaller than Hespeler and when they got here they just didn't know how to adapt and they ran wild. It was just that; ran the streets until all hours. They would work shifts, they would get off at 11:30 at night and they would race all around town and up into the restaurants.... People just wouldn't approve.[21]

Loretta

It was Loretta's turn at bat. She'd been studying the pitches the local Hespeler girl had thrown out, and she was ready to be choosy about her swing target.

Loretta was always up for a game of softball, whether it was an official team from work or just a pickup game with whoever was around the residence, and whatever local girls wanted to play.

It may have been a casually arranged game, but the hard stares from the other team meant she couldn't exactly call this a friendly match. Local girls, who lived at home with their parents, thought the mill girls were wild, and if the mill girls weren't careful, one of them would steal their boyfriend. The mill girls thought the local girls were stuck up and that they thought of themselves as too good to hang around the work-hard, party-hard mill workers.

Anytime there was a chance for the mill girls to show their superiority to Hespeler girls, they took it, even in a hastily arranged softball game.

Loretta had grown up playing sports at home in Corner Brook. In the winter, she had laced up her skates and played hockey on the frozen ponds with the boys, and in summer, she'd kick a soccer ball or throw a softball with whomever was around to play a game. The Hespeler girls, with their organized teams and longer softball seasons, may have thought they knew how to play the game, but Loretta had played in all kinds of weather—rain, cold, gale force winds—and against a range of opponents, including small children and grown men.

If she got good contact between ball and bat on the next pitch, Loretta was certain she could make her way around the bases before the Hespeler girls could tag her out.

The pitcher let one fly. Loretta swung.

CRACK!

The ball flew way out into left field, with the two outfielders racing after it. Loretta rounded first base, then second, then tagged third just before the third base player caught the ball, then fumbled, then dropped it. Loretta took off like a wild rabbit and slid into home plate.

"SAFE," yelled the umpire, a middle-aged man who worked at the washing-machine factory.

Loretta tossed her hair, wiggled her bum, and then strutted from home plate back to her team, her girls from the mill.

18

The Mystery of Loretta, Part 1

It wasn't just Dominion Woollens and Worsteds which photographed the mill girls. Many of the girls and their friends bought their own cameras. They enjoyed taking photos of themselves and their friends as they hung out on the lawn in front of Winston Hall, on excursions to the beach and nearby towns and showing off their latest fashions. It's through some of these photos that the clearest picture of Newfoundland mill girl Loretta Normore emerges.

Like most of the mill girls, Loretta made time for fun outside her shifts. She was part of a girls' softball team. In a team photo, Loretta is wearing a fashionable, vertically striped blouse and pleated pants, leaning slightly on a bat. Other photos show her clad in dresses and well-tailored, double-breasted coats, posing in front of a shop window and in front of a church.

Then there is a photo of Loretta standing between two handsome young men, sharing cigarettes and a laugh. Another shows Loretta and one of those young men in front of a fence in what looks like

A DW&W Industrial League softball team. Loretta Normore is third from the left. Photo by F.C. Hutchings.

a Newfoundland landscape with an uneven wooden fence, spruce trees, and a rocky hill in the background.

But behind her wide smile and her warm laugh, Loretta Normore held secrets. Neither of the young men with Loretta in those photos is Roland Hartung, the man that Loretta married.

Loretta was born in Corner Brook in 1926. Her parents, Sarah and Elijah, had moved to Corner Brook from Little Bay Islands and Sunday Cove, both small fishing communities off the northeast coast of Newfoundland. Sarah and Elijah had taken jobs at the new paper mill in Corner Brook, which was where they met.

By Newfoundland standards of the day, the Normores were a small family. Loretta had one brother, Harvey, and two sisters, including Gladys, Pearl's mother.

Pearl Blanchard, Loretta's niece, is an 82-year-old retired pharmacy manager and trainer. She followed in her aunt's footsteps two decades later. Pearl left Corner Brook in 1962, when she was 20, and moved to Toronto, where she still lives as of 2025. Toronto and Kitchener are only a 90-minute drive from one another. Pearl and Loretta, then married, became close to each other. Loretta was a support to Blanchard as the young woman was building her life in Toronto.

"She was a very jolly person," Blanchard describes. "And very well up on style."

Loretta had been recruited in Corner Brook to work at Dominion Woollens and Worsteds in the mid-1940s, but apart from that, Blanchard doesn't have many details about that period of her aunt's life, except that Loretta wasn't the only member of her family to move away from Newfoundland. Loretta's brother left Corner Brook as a young man, moved to western Canada, and rarely came back.

In Hespeler, Loretta was first assigned to the spinning room. Later, she likely worked with finished fabric. After a few years at the mill—Blanchard isn't quite sure how many—Loretta met Roland Hartung. Loretta and Roland were married in the early 1950s and moved to nearby Kitchener, where Roland had a job at the BF Goodrich tire manufacturing plant. There, Loretta and Roland bought a house and raised their family.

"She wouldn't go anywhere unless she was all dressed up. I never saw her in a pair of slacks," Blanchard recalls.

By the time Blanchard moved to Toronto, Loretta was working in retail sales at a Kmart department store in Kitchener: "If you walked into the store, you could hear her laugh." Blanchard remembers

Loretta bustling around the camera department at the back of the store, with her glasses pushed up on her dark curly hair. Loretta was always decked out in a fashionable dress, cut to flatter her figure.

But behind the bright exterior, what was Loretta holding back? Loretta and Roland had two boys and two girls. It was quietly known within the family that Roland was not the biological father of Debbie, the oldest girl, but Roland had formally adopted her.

Was Debbie's father one of the handsome cigarette-smoking young men in that picture?

"She never talked about anything," Blanchard says. "Things that happened, I didn't know anything about. She took so much to her grave."

Eileen

Eileen ladled out bowls of piping hot moose stew. Gordon was just home after a long shift at the Bowater Mill, and the children were climbing up in his lap, telling him about the exciting things they had done that day. She sighed with contentment. She had definitely made the right choice to come home.

When she left Dominion Woollens and Worsteds in late 1945, Eileen was of two minds. Should she have stayed on? After more than a year, she was getting into the swing of work and life in Hespeler. She had friends and a comfortable residence room to live in, and if she and Gordon went their separate ways, well, there was no shortage of eligible young men.

Eileen fell easily back into the rhythms of life in western Newfoundland—bundling up for the long, snowy winters, berry picking in the summer, and raising six children. She even set rabbit slips in the fall with her brothers.

Her time in Hespeler was beginning to seem like a dream.

Here, in her home in Corner Brook, with the steam from the mill rising above the bay, it was hard to believe that she'd ever lived in that girls' residence, in that pretty town, surrounded by southern Ontario farmland. Not that she ever had much time to think about it. Life was just too busy.

Occasionally, when Eileen spotted a woman wearing a new woollen coat on West Street or saw a basket of imported rock-hard unripe peaches in the grocery store, she thought about what her life might have been like had she stayed in Hespeler. She had several letters in her dresser drawer from her former employers, praising her work and assuring her that, should she ever want to return to Hespeler to work at the mill, there would be a job for her.

But life in Corner Brook was full, with Gordon and their six children. Perhaps, when the children were older, Eileen could go away for another little adventure, a shorter one, perhaps.

Then, Eileen and Gordon would go together.

19

Eileen Goes Home

Eileen had been on night shifts for 13 months when she decided to buy a ticket back to Newfoundland. Working at night and trying to sleep during the day was exhausting, and when she was extremely tired, she missed home more. Christmas was coming, and if she stayed, it would be her second Christmas away from Newfoundland. Her boyfriend, her beloved Gordon Hiscock, had just been discharged from the navy. She needed to see him. She needed to know what was to become of their relationship.

Eileen put in her notice. The company, sorry to see her go, furnished her with a letter of recommendation:

> December 3, 1945
> This is to advise that the bearer, Miss Eileen Penney, was among the group of girls the company engaged in Newfoundland to work at our Hespeler Mill. She now leaves her employment of her own accord

having worked here for the past 13½ months. During her period of employment, we found her to be a very conscientious employee and an efficient machine operator. We have no hesitation in recommending her services in a like capacity to any firm requiring same.

Yours very truly,

Dominion Woollens and Worsteds Ltd.

And so Eileen began another long journey, the reverse of the journey she had taken 13 and a half months previously. She may have travelled home with friends or cousins who were also leaving the mill, as her tickets referred to "Miss Penny and party."

The group went by Canadian Pacific Railway from Galt to Toronto, then Toronto to Montreal, followed by the final mainland Canada leg of Montreal to North Sydney. There they boarded the ferry and steamed across the Cabot Strait to Port aux Basques. Then another train, this time the narrow-gauge Newfie Bullet which hummed along the Newfoundland Railway, to Humbermouth, just outside Corner Brook.

When Eileen stepped off the train in Humbermouth, she and Gordon were finally reunited after more than three years apart. Many mill girls left Dominion Woollens and Worsteds after a year or two, but most stayed in Ontario, to work or marry. Eileen, at 20, was one of the few young women recruited by Dominion Woollens and Worsteds who chose to return home and make a life in Newfoundland.

Eileen and Gordon married two months later, in February 1946.

But Eileen's old employer hadn't forgotten her. She received several more letters of recommendation in the mail, as well as a job offer should she want to return. She was obviously well thought of by her Hespeler employers.

However, Eileen was not interested.

"She always said [that] she made this decision of her life staying home because, of course, my parents were married for well over 50 years," says Gullage. "But I think my mother would have liked to have worked more. There were six children in our family, so she had to be a stay-at-home mother. I think, like a lot of women of her time, [she] would have liked to have had a job outside the house as such. But I don't think she had any great regrets."

Eileen and Gordon chose a quiet domestic life in Corner Brook, but it was one that took adjustments for both of them.

Eileen still thought of her experiences working in the noisy woollen mill and the fun with her friends at Winston Hall and gallivanting around Hespeler on their time off. Gordon, meanwhile, was processing darker memories.

"My dad came home from the navy and he'd had some terrible experiences," Gullage explains. "He was on three boats, those corvettes. And he had three of those sunk out from under him. He was in the North Atlantic for many hours before he was rescued. [He] came back and within a week he was back working at the Bowater Paper Mill in Corner Brook. You wonder how they could really do it, and I guess for the women, too, they got on with it."

Both Eileen and Gordon, through their experiences away from

Newfoundland, had gained an appreciation for being part of a community. For Gordon, that was the camaraderie of being in the navy; for Eileen, living and working among a large group of young women. They took that sense of communal living and responsibility with them into their new lives in Corner Brook.

Eileen took courses in First Aid and Red Cross safety and she was a member of the Legion and the Ladies Auxiliary of the Royal Canadian Legion. Gordon, an electrician at the paper mill, was president of his workplace union and of the Legion.

Eileen's outgoing personality and sense of fun—which had served her well during her time as a mill girl—also served her well as a mother. According to Gullage, "She was young at heart. Winters, [our parents] would take us off somewhere where we could have a really good hill and they would take us sliding, which a lot of our friends' parents never did ... And they went to all the dances and jived and all that kind of stuff. They were great parents."

Still, Eileen rarely talked about her life as a mill girl: "She just got on with it."

Post-World War II, those who served in the military were often remembered, even celebrated. It didn't occur to Eileen to think of her time working at Dominion Woollens and Worsteds as something to be commemorated. She had simply gone to Canada to work for a year or so, then came home. Why would anyone be interested in hearing about her working in a factory? Except for her daughter, no one really asked her.

Loretta

Ah-OO-ga! Ah-OO-ga!

Stan Stoddard pulled up outside Gordon Hall in his 1924 Model T Ford. Compared to the sleek 1940s automobiles that most of the Hespeler boys drove, Stan's rattly vehicle was just one step up from a horse and carriage. Stan made it even more ridiculous by removing the roof and canopy, painting the doors and sides of the car in bright colours, and adding the sign "Ritz Taxi" on the passenger door. And, in case anyone didn't get the joke of his outdated car, on the rear passenger door he'd painted the words "Don't laugh—it's paid for. Is yours?"

Stan's rundown, unfashionable Model T proved to be irresistible to the Gordon Hall girls. They piled into the car any time Stan pulled up, grinning from ear to ear, behind the wheel, ready to drive them wherever they wanted to go. And wherever they chose to go was where the fun happened.

"Come ON, Loretta. Come out to the lake with us." Mary, already

settled in the back seat of the Model T, was referring to Puslinch, the nearby shallow lake. Its trucked-in sand made it a popular swimming and boating area for young people in Hespeler and the surrounding towns.

Loretta paused. She could use her day off to wash her nice sweaters in the sink, take a nap, read her new magazine, and maybe write that long overdue letter to her mother and father in Corner Brook. But then again, many of the Gordon Hall girls would be at Puslinch Lake. She could nap on the beach and have a cold beer or two while she flicked through her magazine. And if she boarded Stan's Ritz Taxi, she would already be at the centre of the party. Someone always had a mickey of whiskey. Stan's buddies waited for them at the beach, ready to admire Loretta and her friends' fashionable swimsuits.

Still, Loretta wasn't convinced. It had been a long week on the mill floor, and her aching arms and shoulders told her she should rest. But then again, if she hopped in the back seat of Stan's car, that would be something to talk about with the girls when they went back on the night shift.

Ah-OO-ga! Ah-OO-ga!

"Hey Loretta, it's now or never—the Ritz Taxi is about to depart," yelled Stan.

Loretta made her decision. Laundry and letter writing could be done anytime. She grabbed her swimsuit, sunglasses, kerchief, magazine, and beach towel. She ran out the door of Gordon Hall and climbed into the back seat.

"To the beach, Stan!"

20

Gone to Hamilton

The spare time with no responsibilities and the freedom that came from living away from the prying eyes and expectations of families was liberating for the mill girls. They flourished within the structure of work and life at Dominion Woollens and Worsteds, and they revelled in the male attention. Photos from private collections belonging to the mill girls' families show the young women enjoying all the hijinks they could get up to when they had friends who were just as game for adventures as they were.

Stan Stoddard, a young man from Hespeler, was a regular presence around Winston Hall. Painted on his souped-up 1924 Model T Ford—an antique automobile even for its time—were the words "Ritz Taxi"; on the rear passenger door, "Smoking area." Stan constantly ferried young mill women to wherever they wanted to go: the beach at Puslinch Lake, the dance halls in Preston and Galt, or the next party.

"Stan and his friends looked like they did a lot of dating over there," comments Turner. But there was a dark side to all this freedom. Decades after the heyday of the mill, Turner remembers people whispering about mill girls who had become pregnant, although no one ever addressed the issue openly. The mill girls he met decades later talked about working on the mill floor and hearing that one of the girls had left suddenly but had not gone home to her family. Or, a girl had abruptly left work, then returned a few weeks later, with no explanation. Considering the wild times that some of these girls had, accidental pregnancies would have been fairly common, and backroom abortions likely happened, although rarely were they talked about.

Turner remembers a Roman Catholic home for unwed mothers in Hamilton, Ontario, an industrial city about 40 kilometres away from Hespeler, on Lake Ontario. He suggests that some of the mill girls went there when they disappeared without explanation for a few weeks. There, they could stay, give birth, put the baby up for adoption, recover, and eventually return to the mill floor, without babies.

Turner, Spring, and the mill girls' children all agree that for decades the mill girls were reluctant to reveal much about their lives or the lives of their friends when they were working at the mill and staying in residences.

Loretta Normore kept her cards close to her chest.

21

Mill Girls without the Mill

Dominion Woollens and Worsteds hit its peak employment and output in the late 1940s. Its largest workforce was in 1949, when 1,557 people worked there.[22]

Even though the days of wartime production were behind them, the postwar economic boom kept the mill's textiles in high demand. The finest men's suits at Holt Renfrew and other high-end Canadian department stores were made with cloth from Dominion Woollens and Worsteds, as were women's dresses and overcoats. The mill also branched out into draperies and upholstery.

Recruitment in Newfoundland was still in full swing. Dominion Woollens and Worsted recruiters continued to scout out clotheslines in central and western Newfoundland for homes with young women, young women with an adventurous streak or who wanted to escape small and crowded houses.

But as the 1940s gave way to the 1950s, the mill's fortunes changed. Lower-cost imported textiles proved attractive to Dominion

Woollens and Worsteds' big customers. New synthetic materials such as plastics and vinyl began to replace the need for woollen clothes. Polyester became more popular than wool for the latest fashions. The company gradually downsized to about 500 workers near the end of the 1950s.[23] In 1958, it went into receivership. It was purchased by the textile company Silknit, which continued operating part of the plant into the 1980s, making smaller-scale modern textiles, until it, too, went into receivership, in 1984.

The mill girls weren't particularly bothered by these changes. Most of them worked for a short time at the mill—a year or two—before they were exhausted by the work and the whirlwind social life and looked for other work or married local men and started families.

The demise of the mill didn't create the worry that the shutdown of a large employer would have created in Newfoundland, where other jobs were scarce. Southwestern Ontario offered plenty of jobs at other

Unidentified workers in the top manufacturing room, 1943. Photo by Frank Johnston, courtesy of Hespeler Heritage Centre.

factories and in the growing automotive manufacturing industry.

Although Eileen went home, Dolly, Daisy, Loretta, and Ella settled in southwestern Ontario, in Hespeler and surrounding towns and cities, and lived there for decades. In the end, they lived for many more years in Ontario than they'd ever lived in Newfoundland.

Although their time at the mill was only a brief part of their adult lives, once a mill girl, always a mill girl.

"They had their own cliques," notes Spring. "When [the mill girls] talk about the people they would consider to be their own, they were the people they were recruited with, the women they resided with in the residences. Those were their friends. They said to me 'when you're sharing dinner, when you're at a dining table with the girls from the mill, those are your friends.'"

The adult children of mill girls remember that their mothers' closest friends were also mill girls from Newfoundland. They called the women "aunt" even if they weren't related by blood. The mill girls, now women, were all "aunties."

Daisy's daughter remembers birthday parties, baby showers, and family celebrations with the families of her mother's friends, all from Newfoundland. Bechtel recalls that it took forever for his mother, Ella, to get through her local supermarket, because she was constantly running into other Newfoundland women who were her friends.

Even though the mill girls stuck together through the decades, seeing each other through life's challenges and joys, their lives weren't about their work at Dominion Woollens and Worsteds, either to them or to their friends and families. Mill jobs were their tickets out of Newfoundland and into a new grown-up life somewhere else.

Their work friendships evolved into adult friendships, about their families, their children, their hobbies, and their shared heritage—being Newfoundlanders and loving the same foods and the same music and comparing trips home to visit relatives. Settled, respectable women in their communities, they didn't like to talk about their younger, wilder days, when they were first living on their own, working hard and playing hard at the mill. Even into their 80s, some stories remained off-limits, even among Dolly and her group of mill girlfriends.

Nicholson remembers "conversations where Mom would just stop talking, put her hand on Aunt Irene's knee, and they would exchange this look. As if they were saying, 'well, we're not going to talk about *that,* are we?'"

Loretta

If you needed to buy a reasonably priced camera in Kitchener in the 1950s or 1960s, Kmart was your best bet. The camera department was at the back of the store, next to the record and hi-fi department.

At the camera counter, Loretta Hartung would be happy to set you up. First, she'd quiz you, with her broad disarming smile, on how you planned to use your camera: Are you a nature photographer? Do you like taking closeups? Are you hoping to take photos of your darling children during the milestones of their young lives?

Then, she'd take a big ring of keys out of her dress pocket and unlock the glass display case below the counter, where fancy Minoltas and Canons for the serious photographers sat alongside Kodak Instamatics—the most popular choice for young mothers who wanted to take photos of their children's birthday parties, first days of school, toboggan rides. Loretta assured young mothers, "I use an Instamatic myself to take family photos, and it works like a charm."

Loretta sent the young mothers on their way with everything they needed to document their precious moments: a Kodak Instamatic camera, an ample supply of 35 mm film and flashcubes, and a coupon for a discount at the store's photo development lab. She waved to them, wishing them good luck and good photos.

Loretta never forgot a face, and every time her customers returned to drop off film for development or to pick up more flash cubes, she asked them about their son's hockey tournament, the twins' birthday party, or their daughter's ballet recital. Over the years, Loretta became a legend at the Kitchener Kmart. Even though her favourite camera was the humble Kodak Instamatic, she knew which make and model of camera each of her customers used, and she even set aside rolls of film for those she knew would want more before the next shipment arrived at the store.

As Loretta Normore Hartung stapled shut small paper bags of film canisters and flashcubes and handed them to her customers or boxed up another Kodak Instamatic camera for a young mother, she often wondered, "Does my John have a family that takes photos of him?"

22

The Mystery of Loretta, Part 2

Rebecca Barker grew up in Cambridge and, as of 2025, lives in the neighbouring city of Kitchener-Waterloo, where she works at a big tech company.

Barker was raised in a blue-collar family, one with tension between her parents, which culminated in a divorce in 1987. As soon as her mother left her family, Rebecca's father, Dwight Barker, drove her and her brother to the Royal York Hotel in Toronto, where they spent a night before boarding a flight to Australia the next day. "[Dad] wanted to get as far away from my mother as possible." Barker returned to Canada after about six months, her brother a year or so later, and her father several years after that.

Dwight Barker grew up in an upper middle-class family in the Preston part of Cambridge. When he was five years old, he was told by his parents that he was adopted. He later told his daughter that he felt like he didn't fit in with his siblings, and despite having material comfort, he never felt fully accepted by his adoptive father. Oddly, he never had a birth certificate, which caused a problem when he was a boy travelling with his baseball team on a trip.

Dwight was told to never search for his birth mother. Barker's grandmother warned her grandchildren: "don't ever, ever try to find your father's birth mother."

When Dwight's adoptive mother, Margaret Jean Barker, died in 2013, Rebecca's curiosity grew. On her father's behalf, she requested his birth certificate from the Ontario government. In March 2016, the birth certificate arrived, and she received some answers.

What she found was curious. Dwight Barker had been born in 1951, in Hamilton, and named John Normore. The mother was listed as Loretta Normore, who was recorded as being Scottish. Gordon Hall was mentioned on the birth certificate; at that time, Barker thought Gordon Hall was someone's name. But at least she had the name of her father's biological mother—Loretta Normore.

"It felt like winning the lottery."

There was more information. Instead of being adopted immediately after birth, John Normore remained with his mother, Loretta, until he was about one month old. Then, young John was sent to a Children's Aid care facility until he was two years old. Dwight had always been told that he was adopted shortly after his birth, but his adoptive family had no photos of him until he was two years old. At the age of two, he was adopted by the Barkers in Preston and given the name Dwight.

Rebecca Barker now had more questions than answers. Why had John/Dwight been taken from his mother? Where did the baby boy and his mother live for the first month of his life? Who was Gordon Hall?

Suddenly, strange stories from her father's childhood made sense. Barker remembers him talking about a time that the Barker family had to suddenly leave Preston for two weeks. His mother explained that "someone is looking for us." Barker needed to find out more about Loretta Normore, Dwight/John's birth mother. She scoured old photos and conducted archive obituary searches, trying to find out anything about the woman who'd given birth to her father.

Then, in June 2016, she read a story in a local newspaper, the *Waterloo Region Record*, about the mill girls and the work that Lary Turner and the Hespeler Heritage Centre volunteers were doing to find out more about them. In that article, Gordon Hall was referenced, but not as a person, as a place—one of the mill girls' residences at Dominion Woollens and Worsteds.

Barker immediately contacted Turner, who obligingly dug through the centre's boxes of material on the mill to see if he had anything on Loretta Normore. He struck gold: Loretta was not from Scotland, as was listed on John Normore's birth certificate—she was from Corner Brook. Gordon Hall, the residence that Loretta had lived in, was still standing, across the street and up the hill from the mill, but it had been converted into apartments. Barker kept looking for more information about Loretta Normore.

"It turned into an obsession. I looked up her name [online] every other day," Barker admits. Yet she never found anything else.

In the fall of 2017, Barker and her partner, Dan, booked a trip to Newfoundland to find out more about the Normore family. She thought that once she arrived in Newfoundland, it would be easy to find people who knew the Normore family, or at least knew the identity of her mother. A few days before their trip, she read an obituary for a man who had died in St. John's in 2016 with Normores listed as relatives. She searched for those names in Newfoundland and Labrador telephone directories and found matches, most in St. John's and some in Corner Brook, and took those names and numbers with her to Newfoundland.

When Barker arrived in St. John's, she called some of the phone numbers on her list. No one answered, and she didn't even get an answering machine where she could leave a message. She was discouraged: "As naive as I was, I thought I would ask around at the pubs and hit the jackpot. That wasn't the case."

Undeterred, Barker worked through her list of phone numbers, this time trying the listings in Corner Brook. Finally, she reached a woman named Trudy. "I think I might be related to you."

They flew to Deer Lake, the airport closest to Corner Brook, where Trudy was waiting to meet them. Trudy looked like family.

"That's exactly how I pictured her," Barker states.

Trudy hugged and kissed Barker and Dan and showed them the photo albums she had brought with her to the airport. Barker had finally found Loretta's family.

Trudy brought Barker and Dan to Corner Brook, where she was introduced to some of Loretta's relatives. Barker was struck by the

Normore clan's physical resemblance to her and her father, Dwight. They all had the same blonde hair, the same smile, the same eyes. She finally had answers.

Loretta had had another child out of wedlock, a girl, Debbie, who stayed with her. When Loretta met and married Roland Hartung, he legally adopted Debbie. The Hartungs had three more children, two boys and a girl. And oddly, Loretta had always been vague about her own age. Loretta was born in 1926, but she often told people that she was a few years younger than she actually was.

Trudy also connected Rebecca with Pearl Blanchard, Loretta's niece in Toronto.

Upon her return to Kitchener-Waterloo, Barker found a cemetery plot in the city for Loretta Hartung, who had passed away in 1999. Her grandmother's final resting place.

Barker had finally solved most of the mystery of Loretta, and she shared what she knew with her girlfriends one day at her home in Kitchener-Waterloo. What must it have been like to have been young and single and pregnant in Hespeler in the 1940s, far from family? How hard must it have been for Loretta to give up her baby boy? As the women talked, they smelled burnt rubber. Barker did a quick check of her house. She hadn't left the stove on; there was nothing wrong with her electronic devices. No one in the neighbourhood was having a backyard fire.

Barker and her friends joked that the spirit of Loretta's husband, who had worked at BF Goodrich, might not have liked their digging into his wife's past.

Ella

Ella brushed the crumbs off the breakfast table, tied shoelaces for her three little boys, then shooed them out the back door to play with their friends in the neighbourhood. She had at least three hours until they came back for lunch, and she was going to steal some of her housework time to tend to her tomato plants.

From the time Ella arrived in Hespeler to work at the mill, she was fascinated by the selection of delicious fresh fruit and vegetables at the mill residences, for sale at local shops and growing on her in-laws', the Bechtels', farm. Tomatoes were one of her favourites. When she was younger in St. John's, macaroni and canned tomatoes was an occasional special at the canteen in the hospital where she worked, but here, she constantly marvelled at the fresh tomato varieties around her, bright red and exploding with flavour. Early Girls, Cherry, Beefsteak. Ella dug into her childhood memories of growing potatoes and cabbages in the garden by the cold north Atlantic Ocean in Carbonear and combined that with the gardening tips she had picked up from her mother-in-law. Ella was going all out growing tomatoes.

Talking about tomatoes and fussing over their outdoor tomato plantings and indoor pots gave Ella a shared interest with her mother-in-law and an easier way to spend time around each other rather than trying to force conversations all the time.

Ella was determined that this year's beefsteak tomatoes would be her biggest and tastiest ever. As she checked the leaves of the plants for insects and decided how much water they needed, she forgot about the laundry, vacuuming, and cooking.

Sometimes, when she was tending to her tomato plants, Ella thought about the mill, just several hundred metres down the street—not that she wanted to be doing that hot, noisy factory work again. She wondered what the current crew of girls working the large, wrought-iron machines were doing at this moment. Were they rushing to keep their daily quota? Were they on their tea break? What plans did they have for when they finished their shift? A softball game or a trip to the beach?

Ella smiled and sighed. Enough with the plants and the memories. She had laundry to hang out and lunch and supper to plan. The three boys were growing like weeds, and her husband, John, would be, as her mother had often said, gut founded by the time he came home for supper after a day on the farm.

23

Ella Makes a Choice

Ella Powell was enjoying life in the prosperous town of Hespeler in the late 1940s. She enjoyed buying new dresses and shoes at the well-stocked clothes shops, and there was always something to do: skating at the rink in the winter, excursions to nearby beaches in summer, all the scheduled activities that the company had to offer.

Ella kept memories of those years through a series of photos that she and her friends took with their cameras—smiling and posing with groups of friends, both male and female, summer and winter. Out and about, well-dressed on the streets of Hespeler, at a fairground, posing in a park, arm in arm with her girlfriends in their fashionable winter coats.

She kept up correspondence with her family in Newfoundland, and she sent home parcels frequently—Christmas gifts and fashionable clothes that she had bought and worn in Hespeler but was now ready to pass on to her sisters and friends. Hespeler was feeling very much like home now.

Relaxing in the main lounge at Winston Hall. Photo by F.C. Hutchings.

"I never thought about leaving," she told her son in the 2004 interview. "I was getting pretty good money. It wasn't high, but [it] gradually got better. We had a good time going out in the nights. Gosh, I used to go skating at the arena, and skating in the open air behind a hotel in Preston ... We had a good time. I never thought of leaving."

Ella was a few years older than most of the other girls at the mill, and yet, her younger coworkers were getting married, leaving the mill, and starting families. As the 1940s turned to the 1950s, more men trickled back onto the Dominion Woollen and Worsted factory floor, and the mill was adapting to more modern needs.

Then, Winston Hall, the centre of all the fun, closed.

"That gave the women a sense that it wasn't going to last forever," Bechtel explains. "So I think my mother realized that it was time she had to find someone to marry." Ella had admitted that, during her time at the mill, she was still upset over her last serious Newfoundland boyfriend. But John Bechtel came along at the right time. He was the best friend of Ella's best friend's boyfriend.

John Bechtel was a broad-shouldered man who wore a nice suit and drove a new car. In Bechtel's collection of family photos from the late 1940s, Ella and John wear sophisticated winter overcoats, perched on the hood of his shiny new car. John came from a simple background: a conservative Mennonite farming family, which held a family farm outside Hespeler. He wanted to get away from his father's house and strike out on his own. Ella figured that he came from a good family, which would make him suitable for marriage.

In 1950, Ella Powell and John Bechtel were married in Hespeler. None of Ella's family from Newfoundland could come, but the Bechtel and Powell families had been introduced via letters.

After they married, life became less glamorous. "I didn't really love him," admitted Ella. "I liked him." John Bechtel took over the farm adjacent to his father's farm; it had a rickety old farmhouse that the newlyweds could live in. But the farming community outside Hespeler was separate from the town, and Ella never felt accepted by her in-laws.

As Bechtel points out, "That was where [my mother] drew the line. She refused to move from the town into the countryside. I think

Ella Powell and John Bechtel. Courtesy of Dale Bechtel.

it would have been a step too far backwards for her because she had already become accustomed after two or three years to this nice town life."

Ella Powell from Carbonear was a city girl at heart.

So instead of living in the rickety farmhouse, Ella, John, and their family lived in Hespeler, just a few hundred metres up Queen Street from the mill, in one of a row of small, wooden two-storey houses with front verandas. That part of Queen Street was an idyllic-looking, 1950s suburban neighbourhood. Ella and John had three sons: Donald, in 1952; Dave, in 1957; and Dale, in 1960. When Dale was five years old, the family moved to the nearby town of Galt.

The Bechtels readily acknowledged they did not have a happy relationship. Compared to Ella's warm, expressive family from Newfoundland, John's family was much more reserved: "It was a very

Germanic, conservative culture, so no one really hugged or kissed."

John Bechtel controlled the family's finances. After their marriage, photos of a fashionably dressed Ella out on the town cease to exist. Ella Powell Bechtel settled into being a town-based farm wife, raising her family and helping manage the family farm.

Everyone who knew Bechtel's mother described her as an adapter. Over her years in Ontario, Ella had lost her strong Newfoundland accent, her vowels and consonants blending in more closely with the speech of her Ontario friends and in-laws. Despite the differences between the Bechtels and the Powells, Ella and her mother-in-law bonded over their shared love of gardening. Ella grew tomato plants in- and outdoors. She had learned canning and pickling while growing up in Carbonear, and she and her mother-in-law enjoyed preserving the bounty from the farm.

Ella was the only Newfoundlander the members of the Mennonite farming community near Hespeler could remember marrying into their culture, and she seemed to have found a way to blend her warm, Newfoundland personality with that of her reserved in-laws. She stayed in touch with her family in Newfoundland, and in later years, visits between Ontario and Newfoundland were frequent.

Ella's life had taken many turns, from growing up in Carbonear, to working at the tobacco factory and infirmary in St. John's, to making her way to Hespeler and meeting John Bechtel. She was preoccupied with the present-day challenges of raising her children and navigating a complicated family life. If she was nostalgic at all, it was for her childhood home and siblings in Carbonear.

Daisy

When the youngsters finally went to bed, Daisy Nichols Westwood took her sewing machine from the linen closet, placed it on the kitchen table, and went to work. Daisy always liked to have projects on the go. The Hespeler Figure Skating Club was all too happy to oblige; with dozens of costumes needed for every show, Daisy was their go-to seamstress.

After marrying Ross Westwood, Daisy channeled her boundless energy into her family. When the children, David and Gail, were in school, she took part-time work in the office at Silknit—the company that had taken over Dominion Woollens and Worsteds in 1959.

In her mill girl years, Daisy had turned out room-sized rolls of worsted woollen fabric for military uniforms. Daisy still loved fabric, but on a much smaller scale—figure skating costumes for six-year-old girls. And instead of dealing with miles and miles of khaki drab, now she was having her way with bright pink tulle and sparkly sequins—the brighter and frillier, the better.

Skating costumes were tricky to make—the fabric was stretchy, like swimsuit fabric. Daisy developed a good eye for how a shrivelled triangle of fabric on a hanger would look when it was worn by a person. When it came to making little tutus or princess costumes for young skaters, Daisy used her expertise to cut, sew, and shape the costumes so that little girls could move and twirl comfortably and gracefully on their skates.

Daisy was thrifty, too. She sewed more practical items—school clothes for her children, even cute matching mother-daughter outfits for her and Gail.

Daisy felt comfortable and at home with her little family. Their bungalow had enough space for everyone. Her children each had their own bed in their own room, something rarely heard of in Newfoundland. Gail was in figure skating and David was in a hockey league—with the proper skates and equipment—something that would have been just a dream in Nicholsville, where children skated on frozen ponds wearing hand-me-down blades and wielding sticks cut from a tree.

Life was still busy, now that Daisy had her own family. She had a cozy home full of love and time to take on a few fun projects at night.

Her life was pink and sparkly, just the way she liked it.

24

Daisy Settles Down

Daisy's life in Hespeler after she left Dominion Woollens and Worsteds was as much of a whirlwind as ever. She worked at a series of jobs in the textile industry with different companies; she boarded with families and cared for their children; and she kept up on news of her siblings in Nicholsville and even encouraged several of her sisters to travel from Newfoundland to Hespeler to work. Those sisters later settled in communities in southwestern Ontario.

Daisy herself took her time in getting married and settling down, not without a bit of drama. "She didn't marry the first person who asked her, I can tell you that," says her daughter. "I think he was engaged to someone else."

It was not love at first sight when Daisy literally bumped into Ross Westwood at the Hespeler ice rink. "There was some Sunday afternoon skating and there were large wooden doors that you had to go in and out of to get onto the ice," Hammond clarifies. "Apparently, she was coming off the ice through the door when he was going in and he was in a hurry and plowed her down, knocked her down to get on the ice ... So I think from what she told us, their first words were not quite pleasant, but that's how they met."

Nonetheless, Ross and Daisy struck up a relationship. They married in 1959, when Daisy was 32, and they had two children, Gail and David. Ross eventually became Hespeler's town clerk, a job in which he knew nearly everybody in the town.

Daisy and Ross created a warm and welcoming home, one far less cramped and hectic than the one where Daisy had grown up with 11 siblings. The tidy, 1,000-square-foot bungalow on David Street had a large backyard and was not far from the hulking textile mill buildings of Dominion Woollens and Worsteds.

"My mom was very quiet then," says Hammond. "The mom that I know, the mom that I've heard of when she was a mill girl, is a little different, with all that socializing. Because growing up, she was a devoted mother at home."

Daisy had moved on from her independent life as a mill girl and posing for glamour swimsuit shots in the company newsletter. She embraced domestic life in Hespeler, applying skills she had learned growing up in a crowded household in Newfoundland and caring for all her young siblings. Daisy loved to be busy.

As Hammond remembers, "Mom was a fantastic cook. She did all the canning and preserves and things that seem to be a lost art. For someone who left home as early as she did, she knew how to do all that. She could sew anything. She was a seamstress and made all of our clothes as kids; she sewed all kinds of dresses and costumes for the figure skating club in Hespeler. She would often spend her nights in front of the TV mending socks for local hockey teams. There wasn't a hockey season that passed where you didn't see an entire team's worth of freshly washed hockey jerseys hanging on our clothesline."

Hammond never saw her mother do any banking or handling family finances, but she remembered how she could stretch a tight family budget.

Daisy enjoyed her home life but she also maintained her mill girl connections. Her closest friends were the women from Newfoundland, who, like Daisy, had worked at the mill when they were teenagers. These former mill girls socialized together frequently, bringing their children to play when they were little. Some even bowled together.

While her children were young, Daisy went back to work on both the factory floor and the office at Silknit, the former Dominion Woollens and Worsteds mill, and worked at other manufacturing facilities: "Mom was a worker; she was born to work."

Even though Daisy had assimilated into life in southwestern Ontario in the 1960s and 1970s, there was still some separation from the families who were Hespeler born and bred. Hammond remembers all her mother's friends as being from the mill, and most of them were from Newfoundland: "We grew up with a lot of her friends who were mill girls, and they would get together. I can remember, you know, birthday parties and baby showers. A lot of the women that were our friends were Newfoundlanders ... All the Newfoundland women, they were all my 'aunts.'"

At those events, Daisy and her friends talked about all the fun they had had as children growing up in Newfoundland. They talked about their adventures working at Dominion Woollens and Worsteds, and they made sure, as the years went on, that they continued to have adventures together. While their husbands worked, the women and their children camped at Sauble Beach, about a two-hour drive north of Cambridge on Lake Huron.

In addition to all her aunties from Newfoundland, Hammond grew up in the midst of a second wave of Newfoundlanders who emigrated to the area in the 1960s. Cambridge became known in Newfoundland as a place to find work: "Our next-door neighbours, the Reids, were from Bell Island. Mr. Reid came and found work at Canadian General Tower over in Galt. They moved into a little 900 square-foot, three-bedroom bungalow beside us and they had eight children."

Steel manufacturers, textile factories, automobile plants—all offered jobs on factory floors for hard-working Newfoundlanders.

Dolly

Dolly was walking home from the bus stop after her shift at the Hostess potato chip factory when she spotted the old Dodge with Newfoundland licence plates in the driveway. Not again!

It was another Walsh brother, with two of his buddies from the Battery in St. John's.

The tiny house she had grown up in on Outer Battery Road kept spitting out youngsters. As they became older and larger, the tiny house seemed even tinier. By their mid- to late teens, it was time for the older children to leave the house and strike out on their own, get a job, get married, leave the province to seek their fortune, just as Dolly had done in the 1940s.

Dolly had been the advance party to the mainland. Now, her house was the unofficial hotel for her relatives who came to set up their lives in Ontario. The 1960s featured a new generation of young Newfoundlanders flocking to southwestern Ontario, and everyone seemed to know someone who had an aunt or older sister who had come to Hespeler years ago. Someone you could stay with first to get your feet on the ground.

As Dolly went through her evening's supper plan in her head, she thought back to how her mother had fed all those children in that tiny house, with the wood stove going all day.

Dolly had prepared a big pot of turkey soup, the end of the leftovers from Thanksgiving dinner. With a few extra vegetables, she could stretch one pot of soup into two. The loaves and the fishes and all that. And she did have one loaf of homemade bread left. She could send young Jerry or Patti to the store for an extra loaf of baker's bread to fill up the boys from home.

She would send the boys off in the morning with bologna sandwiches and a pep talk. Job hunting was hungry work, and the better fed the boys were, the sooner they'd be on their own. They were hard-working Newfoundlanders. They could do it. If they needed references, all the prospective bosses needed to do was to call her.

The boys could stay for a few days. By then, they should have work lined up at one of the plants or factories, and they could pool their resources and find a place of their own. Or go to her sister's place on the other side of town and crash there for a while.

If her mother could keep 17 children going, Dolly could certainly keep her brother and his buddies going for a few days. She was a Walsh, and Walshes took care of each other. Plus, Dolly had a lot more than her mother had when she was raising her children: indoor plumbing, an electric stove, and a supermarket at her disposal.

25

Dolly's Waystation

Dolly Walsh never thought she would move all the way from Newfoundland to Ontario only to meet a man from St. John's. But her good friend Irene Maher was dating a handsome Canadian military man, Martin Power, who was based at the Canadian Armed Forces base in Galt. It was 1954, and Canada was about to send its first soldiers to Sinai, Egypt, for Canada's first United Nations peacekeeping role. Martin was about to ship out.

Irene wanted to go to one last dance in Galt with her beau, and, as the trio of Irene, Olive, and Dolly were inseparable, all three went to the dance hall in Galt for an evening of fun and goodbyes to Irene's beloved Martin. As luck would have it, Martin also brought two wingmen to the dance: his visiting brothers, Gerald and Art Power.

The six Power boys had grown up in St. John's, although their paths had never crossed with those of Dolly, Irene, and Olive. Gerald and Art, like Dolly, wanted to leave home at their first possible opportunity. They, too, were from a large family with few resources and they did not foresee their futures being in Newfoundland. At the ages of 14 and 15, Gerald and Art set out to hitchhike to the United States, specifically Manhattan, the heart of New York City.

Gerald and Art, with the help of their thumbs, slowly made their way to mainland Canada, then south into the United States, and finally to an aunt's house in Hoboken, New Jersey, the home of baseball and Frank Sinatra. It wasn't Manhattan, but it was close. While they caught their breath at their aunt's home, sharing a bed and eating hot meals, they heard about jobs on local dairy farms. Art found jobs for the brothers at a farm in Branchville, New Jersey. They then set to work with cows on the farm.

Their younger brother, Martin, also had the family wanderlust. He left Newfoundland for the Canadian Armed Forces. In the 1950s, Martin was stationed at the Canadian Armed Forces Base in Galt, and Gerald and Art decided to visit him. By then, Martin, like many other young Canadian soldiers in Galt, had become friendly with the young, pretty, and independent mill girls in nearby Hespeler. Martin began dating Irene Maher.

At that dance, as Martin and Irene united for one last evening before he was shipped out, Dolly Walsh caught Gerald's eye.

"Let's face it, Mom was a good-looking woman," says Nicholson.

Dolly and Gerald began a relationship. First, it was long-distance. Gerald hoped that Dolly would eventually join him in New Jersey, but Dolly didn't want to leave Hespeler. So Gerald moved to Hespeler to be with his St. John's girl; he secured a job at the Stamped and Enamelled plant, a factory that made enamel kitchenware and the next biggest employer in Hespeler after the Dominion Woollens and Worsteds mill.

Once Dolly and Gerald became a couple, Dolly moved out of Winston Hall and boarded in a home owned by Gerald's friends Gerald and Violet Mallard. The Mallards became their lifelong friends. Dolly and Gerald eventually married, as did Martin and Irene. The lifelong friends were now sisters-in-law.

Dolly and Gerald's first house was a rented row house in Hespeler, next door to the Stamped and Enamelled factory. Dolly stayed home to care for her two young children—Jerry, born in 1956, and Patti, born in 1959. But just because Dolly had settled down into a marriage and children, and her days of hopping on the electric trolley to go out dancing were behind her, didn't mean that her life became quiet and sedate.

"We didn't have a lot growing up, but I also don't remember our house not being full of people," Nicholson points out. In fact, their house was always full with "a revolving door of relatives coming through."

Although better off financially than her parents in St. John's, Dolly and Gerald still didn't have a lot of money and couldn't afford to bring the family home for visits when they were young. They were, however, always happy to support Dolly's younger siblings coming from Newfoundland. Their home in Hespeler became a regular waystation for family members "looking for a better future except joining the army or fishing."

According to Nicholson, many of Dolly's younger siblings found making a living for themselves in St. John's in the 1960s and 1970s a struggle. There weren't many jobs other than fishing for people who didn't have a formal education. As the mine on nearby Bell Island had shut down, throwing thousands of miners out of work, many young people were competing for scarce jobs.

But the Walsh brothers had an out. Thanks to their big sister Dolly's relocation to southwestern Ontario, and her generous nature, they had a home where they could temporarily lay their heads while they looked for work and got on their feet. Several other Walshes found jobs in the factories around Hespeler, Preston, Galt, and Kitchener. Dolly, like her mother, stashed her visitors wherever she could to sleep. Most often, Dolly's children were told to vacate their beds and sleep on the couch.

"We were small—we could do it."

By the time the children were in school, the family had moved to a slightly bigger house in Preston, with two bedrooms upstairs and a downstairs that consisted mostly of a kitchen—not unlike the house in which Dolly had grown up. Dolly always remembered her upbringing in that crowded small house as magical, and she admired how her mother was able to feed and house so many children. Like many mill girls, Dolly had a knack for thrift; according to Nicholson, "I've never seen anyone make money last like [her]."

Throughout her childhood, Dolly's children continued to vacate their beds for incoming relatives, and Dolly always made sure that everyone had a hearty meal in their bellies.

Dolly and Gerald Power were not the only family of expatriate Newfoundlanders to constantly take care of houseguests. Other former mill girls' homes became places for Newfoundland relatives to land once they arrived in southwestern Ontario by airplane, train, car, or thumb. Like the mill girls in the 1940s, the 1960s' generation of young Newfoundlanders was looking for jobs, a change of scenery, and a better life.

26

The Biggest Outport without a Wharf

Dolly and Gerald Power welcomed a constant stream of siblings, aunt and uncles, and cousins and friends from Newfoundland. Some were simply visiting, on a grand tour of all the relatives who had moved to Ontario, but many were starting new lives in Ontario themselves. The area's manufacturing industry was booming and well-paid jobs—where the main requirement was a willingness to work hard at physical labour—were plentiful. Those jobs were ideal for many young Newfoundlanders.

The mill girls who settled in southwestern Ontario had inadvertently started a Newfoundland expatriate community, one that kept growing by word of mouth. First, it was the mill girls' close friends and relatives who arrived in the Hespeler area, a mini-Newfoundland exodus heading to Upper Canada.

Mill girl Ella begged Mildred, her close friend from St. John's, to come to Hespeler. "After a year or so, she convinced Mildred to come down and join her," remembers her son. "Mildred worked at the mill as well and also married a local boy. They were lifelong friends and we visited them, they visited us, we played with their children."

Then, close friends and relatives of those close friends and relatives began to arrive. Gradually, during the 1950s, more and more Newfoundlanders trickled to southwestern Ontario. In the 1960s, this trickle turned into a raging river. By 1966, the closure of the iron ore mines on Bell Island had put thousands of men out of work. Bell Islanders had heard that many Newfoundlanders worked for good wages in factories and automobile plants in the Hespeler, Galt, and Preston areas and that those industries were hiring.

In 1973, the towns of Hespeler, Preston, and Galt amalgamated to form the city of Cambridge. To young Patti Nicholson, it sometimes seemed that most of the Newfoundlanders coming to Ontario were coming to Cambridge, specifically, coming to stay with her parents, Dolly and Gerald Power. "On Sunday afternoons, Dad would say 'Do you want to go for a drive?' and we'd wind up at the airport [in Toronto], picking up someone from Newfoundland." At the Toronto airport, she could always tell which passengers were from Newfoundland because of their "cardboard luggage"—boxes filled with delicacies that their relatives couldn't buy on the mainland—"salt fish, snacks, all the food from home."

It's difficult to tell how many Newfoundlanders moved to what would become the Cambridge area in the 1950s, 1960s, and 1970s, but there are some clues. In the 1960s and 1970s, the population of Bell Island dropped from about 12,000 people to just over 3,000. Many of those 9,000 who left went to southwestern Ontario.

A study by Greg Marquis of the University of New Brunswick estimates that in one five-year period between 1966 and 1971, about 25,000 Newfoundlanders, most of them in their 20s, moved to Toronto and the surrounding metropolitan areas, which would include the mill girls' new hometowns.[24]

The new city of Cambridge seemed to be full of Newfoundlanders. According to Bechtel, "We were very aware of the Bell Island community that had come in the late '60s or '70s. I remember there was a Bell Islander who was missing his two front teeth and his name was Sid. I don't remember his last name but I think he was doing odd jobs for my dad. He was always at our house and always trying to make bets with me for a dollar."

Daisy's closest friends were all Newfoundlanders who worked at the mill. Shortly after Daisy took the job as a mill girl, several of her sisters followed her to Hespeler and eventually found jobs and made lives for themselves in the surrounding manufacturing communities of southwestern Ontario.

By the 1970s, more Newfoundlanders lived in Cambridge than in many communities in Newfoundland and Labrador. It was said that one in four residents of Cambridge could trace their roots to Newfoundland—they or their parents were from Newfoundland. The city of Cambridge contained within it a landlocked, industrialized, large Newfoundland and Labrador town. People joked that Cambridge was "the biggest outport without a wharf."

Factory floors, supermarkets, and hockey rinks in Cambridge teemed with Newfoundland accents, so many that anyone with a keen ear could isolate the regional variations and guess whether their workmate on the automotive assembly line was from Bell Island or Grand Falls.

Even as Newfoundlanders with cardboard luggage still arrived at the airport in Toronto at a steady clip, shops and services catering to expat Newfoundlanders were popping up all over Cambridge and the surrounding area. Specialty food shops where mill girls and other expats could buy Purity Cream Crackers and buckets of salt beef. Traditional Newfoundland music could be heard in pubs and bars across Cambridge, Kitchener-Waterloo, even down to Hamilton and the suburbs of Toronto. Harry Hibbs, an accordion player from Bell Island, became a celebrity among the expat community. The Pig and Whistle, a show on CTV set in a fictional pub, became a showcase for English, Irish, and, especially, Newfoundland performers from 1967 to 1977.

The heart of all this action, the Newfoundland Club in Cambridge, was a social organization for Newfoundlanders—a place to connect with people from back home for support and socializing.

Starting in 1971, the Cambridge Newfoundland Club threw an indoor-outdoor garden party. This garden party just off Highway 401 was at its largest in the 1970s, 1980s, and early 1990s. It included not only Newfoundland musical performers, food, and crafts but also a softball tournament and children's event. This garden party became a multi-day festival that attracted expat Newfoundlanders from all over southwestern Ontario.

The mill girls were not completely responsible for starting

this mass exodus from Newfoundland to southwestern Ontario. However, in moving to the area a few decades before the wave of arrivals, the mill girls had quietly set up a Cambridge operating base.

"These women came in, and they established relationships within the community," concludes Stapleton. "They put down roots and Newfoundlanders, I don't want to sound stereotypical, but we do want to go where we feel there are other people from where we are from, people who speak like we speak, know what we know, cook what we cook, accordion music, that sort of thing. Many people went there [to Cambridge] because they had a really strong connection, so these girls became women who then became ambassadors. I think nobody ever sat them down as a group and said 'do you know what you did?'"

27

Lary Turner

It wasn't just young people from Newfoundland and Labrador who came to Cambridge in the 1960s. Young workers from all four Atlantic provinces came to the area to seek their fortunes. Lary Turner was one of them.

Turner had grown up in New Brunswick. As soon as he finished school in 1962, he moved to Hespeler. Like the mill girls, he was looking for adventure away from home. Like the mill girls, he first did factory work—at the Simplicity washing-machine factory, a few hundred metres from Dominion Woollens and Worsteds, on the other side of the Speed River.

Like the mill girls, Turner and his factory buddies enjoyed a few years of being young men about town, single and free of responsibilities.

"I knew a ton of them [Newfoundlanders] in the early '60s," Turner recalls. "There were Walshes and Fitzgeralds and so on. And a lot of them stayed and established businesses."

Eventually, Turner met the woman who became his wife, Shirley, who had grown up on a farm outside Hespeler, and the couple settled down to raise a family. The Turners, married for more than 50 years in 2025, have four children and 12 grandchildren. Turner is an unofficial expert on everything and everyone in the Hespeler part of Cambridge, including the mill girls.

From the 1970s to the 1990s, he was a postal service worker, delivering mail door to door, up the hill from Dominion Woollens and Worsteds, on Weaver Street and Winston Boulevard, and the cross streets neatly patchworked with company housing. "I spent 34 years working for the post office here in this community, and of course working in the post office, you get to know just about everybody."

Turner delivered mail to the fancy Victorian houses on the roads farther up Queen Street and in the new subdivisions that joined Hespeler with the different parts of Cambridge, neighbourhoods that factory workers moved into once they made more money. He witnessed Cambridge's growth and change during those decades—the booming years of manufacturing in southwestern Ontario.

As Turner delivered the mail, he became acquainted with the people at all the houses on his routes, especially those who were at home during the day. The daytime residents were mostly stay-at-home mothers who were raising children, taking care of their gardens, cooking, and cleaning while their husbands worked long hours at unionized factory jobs, mostly manufacturing and automotive related, now located in cavernous warehouses along Highway 401.

Turner knew which of the women had originated in Newfoundland decades ago as mill girls. Even though they had lived in Cambridge for longer than they had lived in Newfoundland, their accents were vivid reminders of their childhoods by the North Atlantic, with their rapid-fire speech and their quirky turns of phrase: "They were hard working ladies. And very loyal to the company and very loyal to their families. Just great people. The salt of the earth, as they say."

He admired Ella Powell Bechtel's garden; he chatted with Daisy Nichols Westwood, who always had a long line of hockey jerseys drying on her clothesline; and he noticed the steady stream of visitors at Dolly Walsh Power's house. He noticed that some houses had cars with Newfoundland licence plates parked in the driveways—friends and family from back home searching for their first factory jobs, bunking temporarily with their Cambridge relatives while they found their sea legs and enough money for rent. Many of the guests had stronger, faster versions of the retired mill girls' accents.

These women, the former mill girls, had come from Newfoundland in the 1940s to escape the drudgery they had watched their mothers endure from working in the home. Now the mill girls were doing the same—staying home, raising a family, and cooking and cleaning, this time as suburban North American housewives. But for these former mill girls, working in the home was much different than it had been for their mothers a generation ago and half a continent away. Most of the women had just two to four children. They had modern bungalows with indoor plumbing, including hot running water, and heat, and they shopped for food at supermarkets and local farmers' markets. Of course, being a stereotypical suburban housewife in the second part of the 20th century had its challenges, but they had it much easier than their mothers did, raising a dozen children or more in a small house without many vitamin-packed food choices.

The mill girls were now women who had time to chat with Turner when he brought the mail. Consequently, he learned about their families, their children's sports, their husbands' work, and their own community volunteer work. The talk, he remembers, was always about whatever was happening at the time, the brisk comings and goings of everyday life in southwestern Ontario.

It simply didn't occur to Turner to ask the women about their lives before they married and lived in their bungalows. Similarly, it didn't occur to the former mill girls to open up to the postman about their growing up in Newfoundland or about their work at the mill in Hespeler. It would be unseemly to engage in such a conversation with the postman. Also, why would anyone want to talk about the past when the future looked so bright?

28

Come Back from Away

Although Dolly and Gerald's immediate family lived in Cambridge, their extended family and friends back in Newfoundland tugged at their hearts. Dolly, Gerald, Patti, and Jerry became the classic "come back from away" family—Newfoundlanders living in mainland Canada who made regular journeys back home.

This scene played out across almost every community in Newfoundland and Labrador in the second half of the 20th century: a large car with Ontario licence plates would pull up in a lane by a small house and a family would spill out, parents with Newfoundland accents and children with flat Ontario vowels, about to be set free to roam for a few weeks.

While their children were young, Dolly and Gerald had saved enough money for a station wagon, a vehicle that could get the four of them back to St. John's for summer visits. Gerald retrofitted the station wagon so that the children could sleep in the back, behind the passenger seats. Dolly and Gerald tag teamed the driving, from their driveway in Cambridge to the Nova Scotia-Newfoundland ferry in North Sydney.

"We only stopped for food, gas, smokes and coffee," recalls Dolly's daughter.

The family splurged for a cabin on the ferry, then drove 10 hours across Newfoundland from Port aux Basques to St. John's—and all the way up the winding roads of the Battery to Dolly's parents' house, almost at the end of the Outer Battery, the station wagon barely squeezing between the houses on the narrow streets.

"If my Nan knew we were coming, she would be leaning out over the half door on the side of our house to greet us," Nicholson reminisces. "We were like royalty."

Even though the Powers weren't well off, arriving in a station wagon, all the way from Ontario, with the edges sanded off their Newfoundland accents and their turns of phrase sprinkled with a few Canadian "ehs," they were exotic Upper Canada birds roosting for the summer on Outer Battery Road.

In turn, the Outer Battery was a novelty for the children. Although all of Dolly's siblings had moved out by that time, the small two-bedroom house, reachable only by footpath, still without indoor plumbing, with its stairs down to the outhouse, was a world away from the Power family house in Cambridge. It was "an adventure," according to Nicholson. "When we were there, we were just feral. Nan would make us breakfast, then we were gone until we were hungry."

Nicholson's playground was the Battery, the steep side of Signal Hill, and the entire east end of St. John's. She and her brother ran with a pack of their cousins and their friends from the neighbourhood, returning home to her grandparents' house when it became dark. They even took part in all the local St. John's summer activities, including the carnival-like atmosphere of the Royal St. John's Regatta at nearby Quidi Vidi Lake. As she remembers, "I got lost at the Regatta almost every year."

Likewise, Daisy Nichols Westwood didn't often get home to Newfoundland, but Nicholsville was constantly in her thoughts. She talked to her sister every day on the phone, and in 1959, when her father passed away, she went home to visit. After that, her visits became more frequent. Daisy's siblings were scattered throughout Canada, and when she booked a flight to Newfoundland, she stopped in Nova Scotia to see her sisters who lived there.

"She probably went home more in her later years than she did when she was younger. I'd say she went home five or six times when she was in her late 50s and 60s," says her daughter. "The last time she went, she was in her 80s."

Daisy's daughter loved staying in Nicholsville: "It was so free. I just loved the fact that ... you could walk to a relative's house and just go through someone's fields and you were there, and it wasn't like a subdivision."

Ella Powell Bechtel, too, visited Newfoundland regularly when she was older, sometimes bringing her three sons with her. As Bechtel remembers, the conversations in Carbonear and Bay Roberts, where many of Ella's siblings still lived, were always about growing up and the activities that they loved to do as children.

On the other hand, Loretta Normore Hartung rarely went back to Corner Brook. She and her niece, Pearl Blanchard, travelled back together for the funeral of Pearl's mother, Gladys, who was Loretta's sister. Loretta's mother, Sarah, had remarried after Loretta's father, Elijah, had died. After Sarah remarried, Loretta never returned to Corner Brook. She was now Loretta Hartung of Kitchener, Ontario.

The mill girls had left Newfoundland by train for Hespeler decades before. Now they were women living in Cambridge and the surrounding, bustling southern Ontario cities. They squeezed as much Newfoundland out of their Newfoundland visits as they could—jigging cod, picking berries, and letting their children run free.

When the mill girls reminisced, they mostly talked about Newfoundland. Over cups of tea or glasses of rum and Coke, the talk was all about their Newfoundland family and friends: their adventures when they were children as well as current family business—aging parents still in the family homes, the ups and downs of their siblings' and cousins' lives, the challenges and joys of raising children.

Why they left Newfoundland in the first place—to take jobs as mill girls—never seemed to be something the mill girls or their friends and families talked much about. No one seemed interested in reflecting on those times. That is, except for Turner and a few other curious, community-minded people in Cambridge and Newfoundland.

29

Valerie Spring

Several decades after Ella Powell, Eileen Penney, Daisy Nichols, Dolly Walsh, and Loretta Normore were mill girls, Valerie Spring was wrapped up in the fabric of her own life.

Spring grew up in Galt, later part of the city of Cambridge, in the 1960s and 1970s—at the time when it was filled with factory workers and a booming manufacturing industry. The automotive factories along Highway 401 were the centre of industry then, but, in the early 1900s, her maternal grandparents had emigrated from England to work at Dominion Woollens and Worsteds, by the Speed River, in the Hespeler part of the city.

Spring's grandfather had passed away before she was born but, while she was growing up, her grandmother ran a fabric and upholstery business. Spring remembers spending her Saturdays at the store admiring her grandmother's projects and listening to stories about her grandmother's early days in Hespeler: "When she talked about the mill, it was always about meeting her future husband there. They met when they were 16 and they were married by the time they were 17. It was always kind of part of our folklore, that the mills were where our [family] history really started."

Spring loved studying history, and in the mid-1980s she enrolled in a Master of Arts program at the University of Waterloo in a new program in public history, where she was one of only seven students. The students were energized by the idea that history was not just the information recorded in public records, about what officials, usually men, were doing. Instead, they explored the concept that everyone is part of history—of all genders and races. History was about anyone who had a story to tell about their lives. According to Spring, "Clearly only the 'great men' in the past had the time and the ability to leave the written word to document their actions: historians themselves were members of this class. The majority of people, struggling for existence, would not have the means to leave behind evidence of their passage."[25]

Spring's history professor, Dr. Kenneth McLaughlin, was documenting the history of the manufacturing industry in Preston, Hespeler, and Galt for a book that would be called *Cambridge: The Making of a Canadian City*. However, historians' usual resources—employee records, minutes from committee meetings, or diaries of prominent people, such as the mill general manager's diary—had disappeared.[26]

McLaughlin's father, who had worked at the mill, knew many former mill managers. Through those connections, McLaughlin identified former mill employees, both male and female, who still lived in Cambridge or the surrounding area.

Spring was inspired by her professor's work; the mill was the reason that her family lived in Cambridge. Even though she had always been interested in her grandmother's stories, she became fascinated by the group of young women who had been recruited to work at the mill in the 1940s: "One of the recruiters said that he was recruiting 10 women a week for three years. When you think about where he was recruiting them from for these small communities, these villages and towns to lose even five women to the recruitment would have a significant impact on the towns they were leaving behind."

At that rate, Spring calculated, between 1940 and 1950 Dominion Woollens and Worsteds must have recruited about 6,000 workers, or about 600 workers per year. That was an astounding number, considering that Hespeler had only about 3,000 full-time residents in 1940.

As Spring learned more, her research topic came into focus: the mill girls. She planned to use a fairly new concept in academia—oral history, which requires detailed interviews with people who had experienced historical events. She would record interviews with as many former mill girls as she could find. At the time, they would have been middle-aged or senior women who had been recruited to Dominion Woollens and Worsteds as teenagers in the 1940s.

McLaughlin put Spring and the other public history students in touch with some of these women, and in 1985 and 1986, she set to work. Building relationships with women Spring wanted to interview about their time at the mill proved to be more difficult than she had imagined: "We sent out letters to women that my professor knew

Valerie Spring. Photo by Heather Barrett.

through his father. When that didn't work, we made personal phone calls to them."

The common responses the women gave to Spring, McLaughlin, and the other students were, "Why would anyone be interested in this? Why would anyone want to know what I did at the mill?"

"There was some trepidation on the part of these women to talk about this part of their past," maintains Spring, who is still not completely sure why the women were reluctant. "They honestly didn't believe that anything they did would be of interest to anyone. I think that they were just kind of taken aback that we would find their story of any interest. I think that they were surprised that anybody 40 years later wanted to know what it was like to come to Hespeler in the '40s."

Spring suspects that some of the women might have wondered what other people in the community would think of them, if they opened up about their time as mill girls: "I think part of it was because their managers were still alive. A lot of the company managers were still part of the community. And I think they just wanted to be careful about what they said to make sure that they weren't saying anything that they shouldn't. I just think that they were nervous about how their stories could be interpreted."

Spring was breaking new ground with her research, but she had to do it carefully. She reassured the women by sending them her questionnaire as she interviewed her subjects for her thesis. She wasn't looking for much personal information about them: "We wanted information about the recruitment process, what they found when they got here, and the impact it had on their life in later years." Her group also let the women review interview transcripts, and she would remove anything the women did not want recorded. Then, she had to make an unusual promise to the women to seal the deal: "the actual recordings would not be available for people to listen to for 25 years. The recordings are now with the City of Cambridge archives and anyone who wishes to listen to those recordings can now, but they couldn't until 2011."

Finally, the women agreed to talk. Spring spent much of 1986 sitting down for tea in suburban Cambridge houses, armed with a portable tape recorder and blank cassette tapes. After pressing *record*, she engaged in conversation with women who still had strong Newfoundland and northern Ontario accents.

Spring and her classmates were the first to conduct in-depth, detailed conversations with the women who had worked at the mill. She had agreed to limit her questions to the women's work there, but once the women started talking, the yarns started spinning, and they gave Spring surprisingly candid insight into their lives. The more they talked, the more she admired them.

Still, there was much more: "why didn't we ask them, 'Where were you from and who did you leave behind? And what was it like to say goodbye to your parents?' And then I realized, we had promised not to do that. We didn't want to be that intrusive."

After months of visiting former mill girls at their homes and transcribing conversations recorded on cassette tapes, Spring finished her thesis "Cute as Buttons—An Oral History of Women War Workers at Dominion Woollens and Worsteds Limited" in December 1986. The title was Spring's way of making a point. The phrase "cute as buttons" was used by male supervisors to describe the young women working on the mill floor—young women who were working hard, and getting paid less, at former men's jobs.

"The girls were still judged on their appearance. Yes, they did the work. They did it well. But they were still referred to as 'cute as buttons,'" Spring points out. "Women are incredibly capable. We're seeing women in fields today that we've never seen them in before. But there still is a judgment made based on their gender and appearance."

The bulk of Spring's thesis centred on her extensive interviews with 16 former mill girls. She contextualized their stories by documenting the labour shortage in Canadian manufacturing during World War II. However, Spring received pushback from her history professors: "Well, there was this kind of attitude of 'I can't remember what I did last week, how can they remember what they did 40 years ago? Their memories aren't going to be clear. They'e going to spin it to make them look good.' [They said] history wasn't about sitting around a table and drinking tea and eating cake."

But in public history, which involves documenting people's lived experiences, tea and cake is the portal to a bigger picture of the past. "When you think about it, history has typically been from the male perspective. And so just show it through a female perspective, using oral history, was a little out of the historians' comfort zone," says Spring.

In documenting the lives of the mill girls, this thesis became a passionate defence of the importance of documenting the lives of ordinary people: "The rationale for oral history emanates from the perspective of trying to understand the lives of the majority. It gives the researcher the opportunity to examine the lives of those forgotten in the past."[27]

After graduation, Spring had a long, rewarding career in city planning with the City of Cambridge.

Decades passed. The mill girls became grandmothers and widows, and they began to pass away. For most of them, their time as mill girls was a slice of their long, full lives, a footnote that was mostly kept as a story or two within their families.

Meanwhile, "Cute as Buttons" sat on a library shelf at the University of Waterloo, one of many masters' theses from the 1980s. That was about as much attention as most people in Cambridge, and back home in Newfoundland, paid to the mill girls.

In the words of Spring, "When they left, they left completely."

30

The Company of Neighbours

Turner had always been interested in the goings-on around Hespeler. It's no wonder that, in 1992, he became an enthusiastic member of the heritage group Company of Neighbours. It began as part of a sociology research project by professors C. Kenneth Banks of Wilfred Laurier University in Hamilton and J. Marshall Mangan of Western University in London. At its peak, the Company of Neighbours included a community drop-in centre, community events, book and newsletter publishing, and a history group that has gathered the largest collection of Hespeler-related archive material anywhere in the world at the Hespeler Heritage Centre.[28]

When Turner retired from Canada Post, he threw himself into volunteer work with the Company of Neighbours. As of 2025, the group's main work is running the Hespeler Heritage Centre, and Turner, at 80, is its executive director. In practical terms, that means every weekday, he arrives there at 9 a.m., flips the door sign from "Closed" to "Open," and puts on a pot of coffee for anyone who cares to drop by and talk about all things Hespeler. The drop-in visitors are mostly seniors with an interest in heritage and memories of their younger years in that part of Cambridge.

It's a majestic place to stop for coffee. The centre itself occupies part of the Hespeler former town hall, a stately, three-storey brick building, with two impressive white columns framing the front door from ground to roof, and the former town's war memorial out front. Constructed in 1917, the town hall shows up frequently in the background of photos of the mill girls as they gallivanted around town.

Inside, the walls of the hallways and every room are festooned from top to bottom with photos and memorabilia. One room is dedicated to the contributions of Hespelerites to wars and conflicts around the world; another focuses on sports, with hundreds of photos of teams and individual athletes: hockey players, baseball and softball players, tennis players and golfers, even snooker players. Photos of the Hespeler Figure Skating Club. Photos of hockey superstar Wayne Gretzky. As a boy, Gretzky played Pee-Wee Hockey in Hespeler, and later, long after he established his NHL career, Gretzky became part owner of the town's hockey-stick factory.

The sports photos include team photos from the town's industrial leagues. Throughout the 20th century, factories and manufacturing businesses sponsored teams for their workers. There are team photos of men's hockey and softball from the early part of the 20th century to the present day. In this sprawling sports gallery are women's teams, too. Particularly striking are the female softball Dominion Woollens and Worsteds teams from the 1940s and 1950s, with bright DWW logos on their uniform fronts. Daisy Nichols appears in the front row on one of these team photos, in her sporting glory, on the same wall as Wayne Gretzky.

The centre's Industrial Room at the back of the building, the largest room, is the former Hespeler town council chamber. It is stuffed with office furniture, bits of wrought-iron equipment, a washing machine from the Simplicity washing-machine factory, enamel cookware from Stamped and Enamelled, fabric sample swatch books from Dominion Woollens and Worsteds, and other bric-a-brac that the centre's volunteers collected from industrial sites along the Speed River, before buildings were torn down or renovated. Each section of wall in the Industrial Room displays photos of Hespeler's industries.

The wall dedicated to Dominion Woollens and Worsteds has photos of the exterior of the mill complex in the winter, photos of the machinery—and in nearly every photo that shows workers connected to the mill, most, if not all, are women.

Photos show groups of mill girls on the factory floor and at work on various machines. Others show the mill girls relaxing at Winston and Gordon Halls. Photos from *A Day in the Life of a Mill Girl,* the recruitment presentation, are part of the collection. Here, on this dusty wall in a large, cluttered room, the mill girls are the stars of the show. It is the only section of the Hespeler Heritage Centre walls where the history on display is mostly about women.

At the front of the building, Turner's office, which used to be the mayor's office, has piles of Hespeler memorabilia on every surface:

photo albums, portraits of mayors and town councillors from past decades, and framed photos, certificates, and posters on the walls. Cambridge citizens who clear out their elderly parents' houses or sort through family estates drop by with boxes of memorabilia to donate.

For a long time, Turner didn't think about the gender divide on the centre's walls. Each person in those photos was simply someone who had lived in Hespeler and had worked at a factory, played on a team, or volunteered in the community. The mill girls didn't stand out as unusual. Many Cambridge citizens had a mother, aunt, or grandmother who worked at the mill in the 1940s and 1950s. Women were simply part of the fabric of Hespeler.

Then, in 2014, Turner was contacted by the manager of the Barking Fish, a local bar and restaurant. As the manager, with other Barking Fish staff, worked to extinguish a small fire in a dumpster behind the building, she found a box of old photos. She thought it might be important and salvaged the box.

Inside were hundreds of square black-and-white photos of young men and women, clearly having a great time, and the landmarks placed them clearly in the Hespeler section of Cambridge. Who were they and what were they doing? The box was brought to the Hespeler Heritage Centre.

The unlabelled box did not indicate its owner. Likely someone had cleaned out a house, decided that the box was of no value, and flung it in the dumpster behind the Barking Fish.

What Turner saw was a revelation.

One by one, centre volunteers examined photos of young men

and women lounging in Forbes Park, riding in a ridiculously painted Model T Ford, posing in front of shop windows on Queen Street, and laughing together outside Winston Hall residence, now torn down.

Turner recognized many men from the community and many women from his mail routes—all looking much younger than when he had known them. Judging by the automobiles and clothing styles, he and the other volunteers guessed that most of them had been taken in the late 1940s and early 1950s.

Turner and Hespeler Heritage Society members went through the photos one by one, writing the names of those they could identify on the backs. It occurred to him that, although the Hespeler Heritage Society had been doing a thorough job collecting the official photos of the various businesses, sports teams, military services, and municipal history, they didn't have nearly as many personal photos, especially personal photos that showed young, single women enjoying themselves, unencumbered by children or family responsibilities. Hespeler commemorated the service of those who served overseas during World War II and served on peacekeeping forces in the years afterwards. But these photos indicated that there was action on the home front, too, and women were front and centre.

The young women in the photos were the same young women who had produced the military uniform fabric at Dominion Woollens and Worsteds. By 2014, many of these mill girls were no longer alive. Turner and the volunteers realized that they should collect more information about these women before the last one died.

31

Bernardine Stapleton and Nicole Smith

Bernardine Stapleton and Nicole Smith both grew up in the shadows of the mill girls but didn't realize it.

In 2025, Stapleton is a 60-something actor and playwright, well known in Newfoundland and Labrador. She has performed in comedies and dramas, on the stage and the screen; she has written plays and books; and she teaches. She has performed on stages in large mainland Canadian theatres and stages in school and church halls in tiny Newfoundland and Labrador communities. Much like the way that rural Newfoundlanders pulled together a living, by doing many different jobs and tasks Stapleton has built a career in the arts.

Like most of the mill girls decades before her, Stapleton is from rural Newfoundland. She grew up in Marystown, a community built on the fishery and shipbuilding. That town's fortunes have risen and fallen over the years, and she has kept track, as she does about the fortunes of life across the entire province, especially for women.

Bernardine Stapleton and Nicole Smith, the playwrights who created the play *Girls from Away* about the mill girls. Photo by Heather Barrett.

Stapleton has written and performed in plays about women working in fish plants, women living with domestic violence and addiction, and ordinary women finding joy in their lives. Her work is built on a foundation of diligent research. After decades of working this way, there wasn't much that could surprise her about the lives of Newfoundland and Labrador women. That is, until she met Nicole Smith and heard her story.

Smith was born and raised in Cambridge, Ontario. The lifeblood of Cambridge, when she was growing up in the 1990s, flowed along Highway 401, and through the large windowless factories that employed tens of thousands of people. Those warehouses along the highway were as much a part of the landscape as the farms that surrounded the Cambridge city limits.

An unseen landscape was also a part of Smith's childhood—Newfoundland: "Growing up, a lot of my classmates would always go out to Newfoundland in the summer to go and visit their family.

They'd say they were from Newfoundland even though they were born in Cambridge."

Smith finished high school, studied theatre and writing in Ontario universities, and built a career in the arts in Cambridge. She was always on the lookout for new ideas, and a big one came to her by way of a casual conversation. Her partner, Marty LaChance, a digital creator interested in local Cambridge history, was helping Turner and the Hespeler Heritage Society digitize their large collection of archive material. LaChance was also interested in the factory buildings along the Speed River and was engaged in research into the largest of them all, the Dominion Woollens and Worsteds buildings. In talking with Smith about his work, LaChance mentioned that the phrase "girls from away" kept coming up in his conversations about the mill and the people who had worked there.

Smith was captivated by the idea of a large contingent of young women who had come from faraway places, decades ago, to work at the mill: "I knew I had to hang on to it until it was ready to be told; because it felt like a big story as well as a local one."

In 2016, Smith travelled to St. John's to take part in the Women's Work Festival, which celebrates the work of women in the arts from all over the world. Stapleton was cast in the reading of a play that Smith directed.

One evening, during a social event at the festival, Smith offhandedly dropped information to Stapleton—the story of the "girls from away," the mill girls.

"I couldn't believe it," says Stapleton. "I didn't know anything about this, and I know a lot about Newfoundland and Labrador. I've done a lot of research, a lot of writing, a lot of reading. So I knew right away this was an incredible story that had zero presence on anybody's radar."

The young play director from Cambridge was on to something.

"During the Second World War, understandably, Newfoundland made great, great sacrifices," Stapleton adds. "But on the other side of that was that particularly in the central regions, for some reason, a lot of young women left. It was more than just a demographic shift, it was cultural, it was financial, it was feminist. They didn't even have a word that said feminist. Because they were behaving like it, even though there was no template at the time."

Now was the time, Stapleton and Smith realized, to tell the story of the mill girls. "What greater collaboration could there be than someone who's established from Newfoundland and someone who is emerging from Cambridge to tell this story?" asks Smith.

They immediately set to work. It was more difficult than Stapleton expected to locate much information about the mill girls in Newfoundland or even find their family members. More than 70 years had passed since the Dominion Woollens and Worsteds recruiters scouted out clotheslines for young women's underwear in rural Newfoundland. "If the stories were passed throughout the families, as people died, the story died with it."

In Cambridge, Smith's first visit was to the Hespeler Heritage Centre, where she met with Turner and started digging through the centre's photos, documents, and artifacts. Then, it was on to the

City of Cambridge Archives, where she learned about city employee Valerie Spring and her 1986 thesis. When Smith contacted Spring about her thesis, Spring responded, “Is this a joke?” Spring found herself repeating the exact words to Smith that the former mill girls had said to her in the 1980s: “Why would anyone want to know about that?”

32

Girls from Away

After several years of research, writing, workshops, and rehearsals, in 2022 Stapleton and Smith's play about the mill girls, *Girls from Away*, was ready for the stage. They describe it as a "memory play," a scrapbook of scenes and memories that tell the story of the mill girls. Timothy Matson and Kiersten Noel of St. John's added songs to the play, and the first production of *Girls from Away* was the mainstage production of the 2022 Kitchen Party Theatre Festival in Grand Falls-Windsor, an area of Newfoundland where, decades before, many teenage girls had been recruited for work at the mill.

The play's main character is Bridey Butler, who, when the audience first meets her, is an old woman, getting ready to move to a long-term care home. Bridey's life story is revealed as she tells Valerie, her granddaughter, about her childhood and teen years in Newfoundland and how she decided to leap into the unknown and travel to Canada to take a job as a mill girl.

The play takes the audience through Bridey's life, from her

recruitment in Newfoundland through her long journey to Hespeler with other young women and their chaperone, and into her life at Winston Hall and on the mill floor at Dominion Woollens and Worsteds.

In dialogue and songs, actors bring the stories of the mill girls to life. They re-enact the young women's work at Dominion Woollens and Worsteds, their baseball and softball teams, the *DW&W News* newsletters, even celebrating Christmas at Winston Hall with a Newfoundland flair. *Girls from Away* shows how, through their jobs and living together at Winston Hall, the girls, many of them strangers to each other at first, become lifelong friends. There is a surprise birth, laughter, tears, and decades of women's lives well lived.

At first, audiences were small; no one in Grand Falls-Windsor knew who the play was about or who the mill girls were. Gradually, through word of mouth, more and more people filled the audience seats. They, too, were surprised to hear about these young women from their home communities, their ancestors, who, nearly 80 years earlier, had taken a chance and moved far away to start new lives in Canada.

Spring, who travelled from Cambridge to Grand Falls-Windsor to see the play, was delighted to watch the well-known stories come to life on the stage. She met the cast and shared some of her knowledge. She also met town councillors who, in turn, shared their insight into the history of Grand Falls-Windsor, home of many mill girls.

Girls from Away brought the mill girls' story to life, and it has made their story larger. Through their play, and the conversations it started among audiences, Smith and Stapleton have continued to discover more about the mill girls in both Cambridge and Newfoundland.

33

Step Up Molly

In April 2021, Allison Lupton was in her kitchen in Cambridge baking yet another loaf of sourdough bread and listening to the radio. It was the middle of the COVID-19 pandemic and her life as a busy musician had ground to a halt.

Over several decades, Lupton, a flautist and singer, had built an acclaimed career in folk music, steeped in the traditions of Irish and Celtic music. The Allison Lupton Band was frequently on the road, performing in folk clubs and concert halls across Canada, the United States, and Europe. Lupton, stuck at home in Cambridge, was uncertain when she could resume her career. As she waited for the bread to bake, a CBC Radio documentary on the mill girls wafted over the airwaves.

"I just stopped in my tracks," Lupton explains.

Lupton, who was born and raised on a rural dairy farm near Cambridge, made Cambridge her home base as she developed her career. Despite spending nearly her entire life near where the mill girls had the run of downtown Hespeler, she had never heard of the young female mill workers from away.

"I love a good story—and I love a song that writes itself," says Lupton.

Lupton immediately sat down and wrote "Step Up Molly"—her version of the tale of the mill girls: "I can just imagine what it was like for these women to leave. How brave they must have been." She decided that the song needed Newfoundland musicians. In the fall of 2023, when travel had resumed after the worst of the COVID-19 pandemic had played out, she traced the steps of the mill girls in reverse—from Cambridge to St. John's.

Then, channeling the can-do attitude of the mill girls, Lupton rolled up her sleeves, tuned up her flute, and went to work. She recorded "Step Up Molly" in a St. John's studio with some of Newfoundland and Labrador's finest traditional folk musicians: Matthew Byrne shared vocals with Lupton and played bouzouki; Andrew Collins, mandolin; Jean Hewson, guitar; Christina Smith, cello; Gerry Strong, whistle; Billy Sutton, accordion; and Stratford-based Justin Rouppel, drums.

Lupton wonders how she could have lived in or near Cambridge all her life and never heard of the young women who kept Dominion Woollens and Worsteds going during the 1940s: "They [the mill girls] just didn't think it mattered?"

By performing the song, Lupton honours the mill girls' remarkable contributions to life in Cambridge.

Step Up Molly[29]

In '42 when all was new a tall man came to town
His coat was fine, his boots did shine, he walked the village round
Young ladies haste! Adventure waits in south Ontario
Work Hespeler Mill, it's such a thrill, sign on the line below

Chorus
Won't you step up Molly, follow me down
Hey, hey Hespeler Town
Weave, spin, up turn around
Step up follow me down

I listened well what he did tell and thought about my lot
Why should I leave Bell Island this eve I asked the Mill big shot
He looked around until he found and set his eyes on me
He said, "You're young! By twenty-one, I recommend a spree!"

"Please take a seat. Something to eat and gaze upon the screen.
This film I know will clearly show the wonders to be seen
All work, no play is not Mill way. There's much to see and do.
Feel inspired? Why join the choir! Play hockey, baseball too."

My cousin Bea and I agreed so kissed our friends good-bye
We sailed away that very day upon the evening tide

At Hespeler Mill we joined the girls and found a place in line
We settled in and learned to spin, wrote letters home to mine

And then by chance they called a dance for locals at the hall
In rings and curls, Bell Island girls sat not one dance at all
But things turned grim when Jim cut in and Michael cleared the floor
Punches flew, the air turned blue, they bolted for the door.

I settled down near Hespeler town with Jim along the Grand
I missed Bell Island and mother's smile so far from Newfoundland
I sent word back to brother Jack and friends who worked the mine
So glad to say some came my way, found work upon the lines

34

Eileen, Loretta, Ella, Dolly, and Daisy: The End of an Era

Eileen Penney Hiscock and her husband, Gordon Hiscock, may have settled in Corner Brook, but their time away—Eileen as a mill girl in Hespeler and Gordon at sea with the Canadian navy—gave them a taste for adventure. They were avid outdoors people, hunting and fishing together on Newfoundland's west coast. Even though they had six children and were active community volunteers, they took time to do things together such as a road trip through the United States. They had a long and happy life together. Eileen passed away on March 7, 1998, at the age of 71; her beloved Gordon followed her 15 months later, in June 1999.

Loretta Normore Hartung's home became Kitchener. She never reunited with her first-born son, John. In 1995, Loretta lost her youngest son, Peter, who died at the age of 31 in a snowmobile accident in Saskatchewan. Still, Loretta appreciated the fun in life. In all the photos of her, Loretta is smiling and laughing, whether she is playing a game of cards or joking around at an expat Newfoundland community gathering. Loretta died in 1999 at the age of 73.

In her later years, Ella Powell Bechtel enjoyed frequent trips to Newfoundland to visit family and friends, bringing her Ontario children with her to discover the finer points of outport Newfoundland life. Even though Ella's elegance is preserved in photos of her dressed in the finest clothes in her younger days, Ella was known to her neighbours and friends in her gardening clothes, tending to the beautiful and bountiful gardens she kept at her homes in Cambridge and then Kitchener. In addition to her famous tomatoes, Ella's geraniums were legendary to her Cambridge and Kitchener friends. Ella passed away on August 17, 2009, one month before her 84th birthday.

Dolly Walsh Power lived a long and rollicking life, always making room for more people at her table; she passed away on June 25, 2022, at the age of 95. Nicholson says that she cooked meals for family and friends a month before she passed. Dolly's obituary photo, the one the family chose to represent her 95 years of life, showed Dolly, the mill girl, operating a large piece of machinery at Dominion Woollens and Worsteds.

And Daisy? Daisy Nichols Westwood, who lived to be 96, passed away in the fall of 2024, a month before her 97th birthday. Known as the Queen of David Street, she lived for nearly 65 years in the tidy house on David Street that she and her husband, Ross, had bought together. Her early days of being a big sister caring for her many younger brothers and sisters in Nicholsville never left her. Daisy was a motherly and grandmotherly figure for generations of children on the street, even becoming godmother to several of them. Until the end of her life, Daisy was busy at something—cleaning, baking, sewing, or knitting a project for a friend or a family member. As Daisy's friends and family members attest, Daisy was always a worker.

35

Cambridge Today

Eighty years from the heyday of the mill girls, Cambridge has a population of about 138,000, and its Hespeler, Preston, and Galt neighbourhoods are linked by a sprawl of highways, shopping malls, and suburban subdivisions.

According to Hammond, Cambridge, especially the Hespeler part, "is a very friendly town. I think a lot of that came with the Newfoundlanders because we already know that Newfoundland is the friendliest place in Canada. That friendliness and willingness to help others."

The young Newfoundland women at Dominion Woollens and Worsteds weren't the only "mill girls" in Canada during the 1940s. At that time, young women from all across Canada were on the move to fill jobs at factories in Ontario and Quebec that had been vacated by men who had gone to war. Cambridge is filled with people of Newfoundland and Labrador descent and heritage, most of whom are most associated with the wave of families who moved to the area in the 1960s after Bell Island's iron ore mines closed, not with the cohort of older female relatives who made that migration possible.

"I think the mill girls are not particularly well known because it's a women's story," suggests Smith. "A lot of the time this story of economic migration and a shift in cultural demographics belongs to men, or that's what we hear. I think it says a lot about what's valued. I think a lot of the time women's stories aren't looked at in the same way, even by them [the women]. Even in Valerie's interviews, you could tell that 20 years, 40 years after these women worked at the mill, they really didn't think they had any impact or anything to share."

In Newfoundland and Labrador today, young people continue to leave and build lives in other parts of Canada and the world, but there are more opportunities for young people to build careers and lives at home. It's still a part of Canada that is deeply interested in its heritage, and culture, yet, the mill girls' story—who they were, which communities they came from, why they left, and where they ended up—is little known.

"To me, it's mind boggling that there is not some sort of registry [in Newfoundland and Labrador]," Nicholson points out.

"They got married, they changed their maiden names to their married names," adds Stapleton. "They weren't keeping records the way we do now. They weren't getting written up in the papers."

Stapleton would have liked to have known about the mill girls when they were still alive, but she's not surprised that their accomplishments and adventures haven't been heard widely: "I think women's stories get eaten up in a patriarchal world."

Nicholson puts it more bluntly. "It's a sexist thing. No one bothered to ask."

Hespeler is now a neighbourhood in Cambridge called Hespeler Village. Queen Street, the downtown main drag where all the action happened in the 1940s, is much quieter. The strip of two- and three-storey buildings, which once housed butchers, greengrocers, medical offices, a post office, and a pharmacy, is now occupied with boutiques, small restaurants, and coffee shops. Most Hespelerites get their basics by driving to big box shopping areas and modern offices off the highways. Farther down Queen Street, past the retail area, the older homes that existed when the mill girls first came to town are now well-kept heritage homes.

The rail line that brought the mill girls from North Sydney to Hespeler still runs between Queen Street and the Speed River, although mostly freight trains use the line these days. Across the street from the original Bucket of Blood, the former Queen's Hotel still stands, renovated and wearing a fresh coat of coral and beige paint. It's now the popular restaurant Ernie's Roadhouse. Where the Glick building stood, with the Bucket of Blood Dance Hall on the second floor, is a four-storey condominium complex.

A few smaller early-20th-century factory buildings along the Speed River have been converted into condos, breweries, and small-scale commercial space. The stately brick municipal buildings of the former town of Hespeler are occupied and used by the City of Cambridge.

Over the years, parts of the mill facility closest to the Speed River were dismantled, and in 1995, a fire destroyed other sections of the abandoned mill. A long, rectangular empty field, stretching south of the remaining mill building, is all that remains of most of the mill complex. Another smaller field to the west runs parallel between the remaining building and the river. If the entire Dominion Woollens and Worsted complex were still standing, it would stretch 500 metres along Queen Street. A small portion of the mill remains—the Number 3 building. Small is relative, as the Number 3 building is a large, brick, three-storey industrial warehouse. There has been talk of turning the abandoned building into condos or offices, but as of 2025 its future is uncertain.

Gordon Hall still stands, with its two stories of balconies, relatively unchanged on the outside, behind a lawn of mature trees, divided into apartments. Winston Hall was torn down in the 1960s, and a small trailer park was put on the grounds. A cluster of older trailer homes still stands on the Winston Hall grounds.

Farther up that hill, the mill girls' homes still stand. The small square, two- and three-bedroom postwar brick bungalows look remarkably close to their original form, still small and centred on large, leafy garden lots with now mature trees.

The town where the mill girls and their friends once ran free and wild in their youth, with an industrial complex operating around the clock, thousands of workers streaming back and forth, and young people playing on sports teams or dancing up a storm, is now regarded as a pastoral section of Cambridge, a quiet area with heritage homes, leafy parks and walking trails, and scenic places to enjoy a meal or a drink. A few historical interpretive panels dot the neighbourhood, telling the story of Hespeler's industrial roots, and the founders of the town, but there is no panel about the mill girls.

"I still think that there is a lot of male dominance in history departments and that I think we still rely on the male historians to tell our story," Spring concludes. "I think that we still have a lot of work to do."

The Cambridge Newfoundland Club is the headquarters of its Newfoundland and Labrador community. Located in the shopping and industrial strip that joins the Galt, Preston, and Hespeler parts of Cambridge, this large, windowless building rents itself out as a wedding and banquet hall to everyone, from Newfoundland and otherwise. It's across the street from a shopping centre, and it's next door to the Armenian Community Centre of Cambridge and the Islamic Centre of Cambridge.

The Cambridge Newfoundland Club's membership is predominantly made up of retirees from nearby factories, not the young single women and men or young families that loaded its doors to bursting in the mid-1970s. The friendly woman from Bell Island tending the bar didn't know much about the mill girls, but she intended to ask around at the club's next seniors' afternoon.

The Newfoundland Club keeps busy with dart leagues, card games, and old-time traditional Newfoundland bands, but it doesn't dominate nightlife in Cambridge as it did a few decades ago. In 2025, Cambridge is a melting pot of citizens from around the world, like most of southwestern Ontario.

The mill girls, who had made such a splash, were so colourful and noisy, and took up so much space, are now quiet ghosts.

36

Children of the Mill Girls

As the mill girls died, many of their stories died with them, unless their children, or someone who was *really* interested in mid-20th-century manufacturing in southwestern Ontario, convinced them to talk about those years working at Dominion Woollens and Worsteds.

"I don't even know if Mom talked about it with my other brothers and sisters," says Gullage. "I did contact them and said, 'Besides what I wrote on the family history, did Mom ever talk to you about it? Or was there anything I missed, that she told you and she didn't tell me?' And none of them had anything."

Gullage thinks that her mother decided to tell her about her time as a mill girl to help her through her own move as a teenager decades later. About the same age as her mother when she moved to Hespeler, Gullage had left her family home and moved east, across Newfoundland to St. John's to attend Memorial University: "Mom probably talked to me about it because when I went away from home, I suffered from homesickness, living in [university] residence."

Eileen's pep talk to her daughter helped her through her homesickness at university, and a few years later, Gullage and her husband settled in Corner Brook to start a family. But also like Eileen and Gordon, Gullage and her husband love to travel.

After their time at the mill, nearly all the mill girls had become mothers. "[Mom] was 35 when I was born and while she was still alive, you just have a child-parent relationship," says Ella Powell Bechtel's son. "You think of them at that moment in time, in the here and now. I really didn't put a lot of thought into what was almost half her life before I was born."

Ella, the go-getter from Carbonear, passed on her sense of adventure to her three boys. Bechtel's two brothers lived and worked in different parts of Canada, and, in 1989, he moved to Europe to work as a journalist. Bechtel had a long career in European public broadcasting and, as of 2025, lives in Switzerland.

Ella supported her sons wherever they wanted to move. Bechtel now understands how at least some of that support came from his mother's determination to go somewhere new, far from Newfoundland.

As a teenager, Nicholson, like her mother, Dolly Power Walsh, was itching to see the world beyond her hometown of Cambridge: "I just knew there were bigger and better things." She studied and worked hard, accelerated her way through high school, and graduated a few months early. The teenager then bought an airplane ticket for England. She travelled and worked in Europe for a few years, then eventually returned to the Cambridge area, attended college, married, and has had a long and rewarding career in adult education.

Although Dwight Barker never did meet his biological mother, Loretta Normore Hartung, some of his actions—his restlessness and his feeling like he never belonged—now make more sense to his daughter. To Loretta, moving from Corner Brook to Hespeler in the 1940s may have seemed like moving to the other side of the world. Forty years later, when her biological son's marriage broke up and he fled to Australia, he actually moved, with his children, to the other side of the world.

The community the mill girls built—that first wave of young women who moved to Hespeler from Newfoundland in the 1940s—followed by a larger wave of Newfoundlanders in the 1960s, created a Newfoundland community around their children, who were all born in Ontario but found themselves surrounded by Newfoundlanders.

Gail Hammond, Daisy Nichols Westwood's daughter, grew up around Daisy's Newfoundland friends, whom she called her aunts, and their families. About one in four people living in Cambridge in the 1970s was either from Newfoundland or had parents who were from Newfoundland. Hammond had many friends who were either from Newfoundland or who, like her, had one or both parents who were from Newfoundland. Her husband, Brian Hammond, is one of them. His parents emigrated from Bell Island via Labrador.

"Brian's father, Bernard, was a barber, the first barber in Churchill Falls, Labrador, and then they [Brian's parents] came here and worked at MacDonald Steel. Many of Bernard's brothers and sisters came as well," Hammond explains.

When Hammond's in-laws retired from their jobs in Cambridge, they moved back to their hometown of Bell Island, where Gail and Brian visit them every three years or so.

As Hammond's generation had their own children, Daisy and the mill girls, now mill grandmothers, were still going on adventures, now with extra company: "Mom and her friends would rent a cottage and take their grandchildren with them [for a vacation]."

Then there are the women who are not related by blood to the mill girls but in trying to find out more about them, and digging into their pasts to find out more about their stories, they feel a deep connection to them.

Spring became acquainted with some of the mill girls 40 years after they first moved to Cambridge. Forty years after Spring's thesis about the mill girls was completed, Stapleton and Smith discovered her work.

"If she [Spring] had not persevered, this story would be gone, poof," insists Stapleton.

"It really thrills me that people are interested in this story, not only from the Cambridge perspective but from the Newfoundland perspective," Spring adds.

37

Another Look at the Photos

The longer you look at the photos of the mill girls at the Hespeler Heritage Centre, the more there is to see. Their hairstyles and clothing are up to the minute for the 1940s, and they still look ready to leap out of those black-and-white squares to take on whatever the current day would bring.

The more you learn about them, the more contemporary the young women's faces look. They could be the faces you would see in Newfoundland and Labrador today, at work, at the mall, or at a concert or a sporting event. They are faces, if you saw them in Cambridge, you might think, *I bet she's from Newfoundland.*

The Hespeler Heritage Centre feels like the true home of the mill girls these days. The building is just down the road from the old mill and where Winston Hall once stood. Turner and the volunteers sort through the mountain of Hespeler memorabilia—a large portion of which revolves around the goings-on at Dominion Woollens and Worsteds, and everyone who worked there. Tech-savvy volunteers

Olive Maher (centre), Dolly Walsh (right), and an unidentified woman. Courtesy of Patti Nicholson.

work on the gigantic task of digitizing at least part of the centre's collection.

A few kilometres away, the City of Cambridge Archives holds a collection of *DW&W News* newsletters, where you can leaf through the latest news of the mid-20th-century textile industry and admire the photos of the mill girls, living their best lives.

When I look at those young Newfoundland women, I wonder, Who is jumping in now to do the manual labour that keeps our country going? Whose work are we not celebrating? Whose stories are we missing?

"I hope we can start thinking about the everyday in a more special way. Everyone has a life full of stories worth telling and worth sharing," insists Smith. "My hope is that their story just travels like the tidal wave and that we can find other stories like this, because there have to be."

Stapleton hopes that somewhere there could be a permanent exhibit, complete with enlarged photos of the girls from away, the mill girls, that tells their story. "Maybe their grandchildren will come in with their great-grandchildren and say 'Oh my God, that was my grandmother. What a gal she was.'"

Endnotes

1 Kevin Swayze, "End of an Era," *The Cambridge Reporter*, April 5, 1989, 6.

2 Kenneth McLaughlin and Kristel Fleuren, with Arlene Doucette, Ronna Ells, and Sarah Sixsmith, *Hespeler: Portrait of an Ontario Town* (The Company of Neighbours, 2006), 24-25.

3 Dalton Campbell, "LAC's Collection of Labour Union Charters," Library and Archives Canada Blog, November 28, 2024, https://thediscoverblog.com/tag/labour/.

4 Kateryna Tonkykh, "Untangling the Knot: A Brief History of the Canadian Textile Industry," *Ingenium Channel*, December 23, 2019, https://ingeniumcanada.org/channel/articles/untangling-the-knot-a-brief-history-of-the-canadian-textile-industry.

5 Valerie J. Spring, "'Cute as Buttons': An Oral History of the Experience of Women War Workers at Dominion Woollens and Worsteds Limited" (master's thesis, University of Waterloo, 1986), 16.

6 Swayze, "End of an Era."

7 Sean Cadigan, "The Second World War, 1939-1945," 2007, Heritage Newfoundland and Labrador, https://www.heritage.nf.ca/articles/politics/second-world-war.php.

8 Spring, "Cute as Buttons," 16.

9 Spring, "Cute as Buttons," 18.

10 Valerie J. Spring, interview by Heather Barrett. All quotations from Spring's thesis are cited in the endnotes; those from the interview with the author are not.

11 Newspaper clipping, courtesy of Lary Turner, Hespeler Heritage Centre. Newspaper name, date, and page unknown.

12 Ruth Hudson and Ted Hudson, "Homeland to Hespeler," *The Atlantic Guardian*, April 1945, 11-14, 25.

13 *DW&W News*, April 1944. Held in the City of Cambridge archives.

14 Spring, "Cute as Buttons," 28.

15 Spring, "Cute as Buttons," 29.

16 Spring, "Cute as Buttons," 45.

17 Spring, "Cute as Buttons," 46.

18 *DW&W Newsletter*, March 1944.

19 McLaughlin and Fleuren, *Hespeler,* 16.

20 McLaughlin and Fleuren, *Hespeler,* 30.

21 Spring, "Cute as Buttons," 32.

22 Barry Ries, "Student Ponders Fate of 'industrial artifact,'" *Kitchener-Waterloo Record,* January 8, 1986.

23 Ries, "Student Ponders Fate."

24 Greg Marquis, "Confederation's Casualties: The 'Maritimer' as a Problem in 1960s Toronto," *Acadiensis* 39, no. 1 (Winter/Spring 2010): 83-107, https://journals.lib.unb.ca/index.php/acadiensis/article/view/15385/16526.

25 Spring, "Cute as Buttons," 7.

26 Spring, "Cute as Buttons," 9.

27 Spring, "Cute as Buttons," 7-8.

28 https://hespelerheritagecentre.ca/.

29 A. Lupton, SOCAN, 2021, with permission.

References

Cadigan, Sean. "The Second World War, 1939-1945." 2007. Heritage Newfoundland and Labrador. https://www.heritage.nf.ca/articles/politics/second-world-war.php.

"Cambridge Newfoundland Club Celebrating Annual Reunion This Weekend." *Cambridge Today,* June 28, 2023.

Campbell, Dalton. "LAC's Collection of Labour Union Charters." Library and Archives Canada Blog, November 28, 2024. https://thediscoverblog.com/tag/labour/.

Dominion Woollens and Worsteds Ltd., University of Waterloo Archives Database. https://archives.uwaterloo.ca/index.php/dominion-woollens-and-worsteds-ltd.

Hespeler Heritage Centre: https://hespelerheritagecentre.ca/.

Higgins, Jenny. "Newfoundlanders and Labradorians in WWII." 2007. Heritage Newfoundland and Labrador. https://www.heritage.nf.ca/articles/politics/newfoundlanders-labradorians-wwii.php#:~:text=The%20first%20draft%20of%20recruits,branch%20of%20the%20armed%20forces.

Hudson, Ruth and Ted Hudson, "Homeland to Hespeler," *The Atlantic Guardian,* April 1945.

Marquis, Greg. "Confederation's Casualties: The 'Maritimer' as a Problem in 1960s Toronto." *Acadiensis* 39, no. 1 (Winter/Spring 2010): 83-107. https://journals.lib.unb.ca/index.php/acadiensis/article/view/15385/16526.

Marsh, Bryan. "Not-Fit Living Conditions in the Newfoundland Lumber Camps." December 1, 2016. Anglo Newfoundland Development Company. https://anglonewfoundlanddevelopmentcompany.ca/2016/12/01/not-fit-living-conditions-in-the-newfoundland-lumber-camps/.

McCullough, Alan Bruce. *The Primary Textile Industry in Canada: History and Heritage.* National Historic Sites, Parks Canada, Environment Canada, 1992. https://books.google.ca/books/about/The_Primary_Textile_Industry_in_Canada.html?id=VgzcAAAAMAAJ&redir_esc=y.

McLaughlin, Kenneth and Kristel Fleuren, with Arlene Doucette, Ronna Ells, and Sarah Sixsmith. *Hespeler: Portrait of an Ontario Town.* The Company of Neighbours, 2006.

Mercer, Greg. "Mill Girls." *Waterloo Region Record,* June 24, 2016.

"Monument Dedicated to Founder of Nicholsville." *Saltwire,* July 1, 2010. https://www.saltwire.com/atlantic-canada/lifestyles/monument-dedicated-to-founder-of-nicholsville-140637/.

Rennie, Rick. "Work and Life in the Bell Island Mines." 1998, updated 2019. Heritage Newfoundland and Labrador. https://www.heritage.nf.ca/articles/economy/bell-island-work.php.

Report of the Royal Commission on the Textile Industry. W.F.A. Turgeon, Commissioner. 1938. Ottawa, Printer to the King's Most Excellent Majesty. https://epe.lac-bac.gc.ca/100/200/301/pco-bcp/commissions-ef/turgeon1938b-eng/turgeon1938b-part1-eng.pdf.

Ries, Barry. "Student Ponders Fate of 'industrial artifact.'" *Kitchener-Waterloo Record,* January 8, 1986.

Slone, Isabel. "Why Isn't More Clothing Made in Canada?" *Macleans,* July 21, 2021. https://macleans.ca/economy/why-isnt-more-clothing-made-in-canada/.

Spring, Valerie J. "'Cute as Buttons': An Oral History of the Experience of Women War Workers at Dominion Woollens and Worsteds Limited." Master's thesis, University of Waterloo, 1986.

Swayze, Kevin. "End of an Era." *The Cambridge Reporter,* April 5, 1989.

Symonds, Richard. "The Architecture and Planning of the Townsite Development Corner Brook 1923-5." The Heritage Foundation of Newfoundland and Labrador. https://heritagenl.ca/wp-content/uploads/2018/01/report-cornerbrook-townsite.pdf.

Tonkykh, Kateryna. "Untangling the Knot: A Brief History of the Canadian Textile Industry." *Ingenium Channel,* December 23, 2019. https://ingeniumcanada.org/channel/articles/untangling-the-knot-a-brief-history-of-the-canadian-textile-industry.

Valen, Dustin. "Commerce, Class, and the Newfoundland Hotel." October 21, 2020. *Society for the Study of Architecture in Canada.* https://canada-architecture.org/commerce-class-and-the-newfoundland-hotel/.

Acknowledgements

There are many people who believe in the story of the mill girls and are determined to keep their story alive. You are part of this story already, but it is your generosity and support of my work which made this book happen.

The children and relatives of the mill girls—Rebecca Barker, Dale Bechtel, Pearl Blanchard, Terry Gullage, Gail Hammond, Patti Nicholson, Marie Peden, and others—thank you for sharing your mothers, aunts, and grandmothers with me and trusting me to share their story with readers of this book. I take that task seriously. Thank you, too, for sharing photos and other documents belonging to your mothers. Your generosity of spirit is great.

Bernardine Stapleton and Nicole Smith: if you hadn't told me about your play *Girls from Away*, I would never have known about these incredible women. Thank you for your generosity of time and information and your passion for keeping these women's stories alive. Thank you, for giving me your blessing to take on this book project. Allison Lupton: thank you for bringing the mill girls to life in song. I am looking forward to your next gig in St. John's!

Lary Turner and the volunteers at the Hespeler Heritage Centre: thank you for your support for this project and for your deep love of and commitment to preserving the heritage and stories of the Hespeler part of Cambridge. Lary, you are an endless fountain of information and you have been so generous in sharing the centre's wealth of information with me as well as its incredible collection of photos. It was a delight to spend time with all of you at the centre. The Hespeler Heritage Centre is a jewel. Marty LaChance: thank you for all your work digitizing the collections at the Hespeler Heritage Centre and creating the amazing Dominion Woollens and Worsteds throwback website and for sharing your knowledge of historical Cambridge with me. Thanks, too, for the ride from the airport!

Valerie Spring: you may never have thought how important your 1986 history thesis would become, but thank you for sharing that thesis and your razor-sharp analysis of the girls and southwestern Ontario of the 1940s with me. Your respect and admiration for these women and their legacies shine through in your work.

Dan Schmalz, Information and Archives Analyst at the City of Cambridge Archives: thank you for your interest in this project and your generosity in making the information at the archives accessible for this project. Your passion for the history of Cambridge is contagious, in a good way. Thank you for recognizing the importance of telling these women's stories.

Susan Flanagan, Trudy Morgan-Cole, and Paul Shea in St. John's were early readers of this project and their excellent advice and guidance kept me going. Thank you to the NL Public Libraries Writers in Residence Program for making Trudy's expertise and encouragement available to me. A big thank you to Susan for her friendship, moral support, and encouragement to "Just get it all down!"

Before this book, I made a radio documentary and digital feature about the mill girls for the CBC. Thank you to CBC and my colleagues there for letting me go down random rabbit holes to pursue stories and for permitting me to use some of my research and interview material from that project for this book.

Stephanie Porter is my excellent editor at Boulder Books. Her ear and eye are crucial to this project. Iona Bulgin and her eagle's eye for detail provided additional editing support. To Gavin Will of Boulder: thank you for your support for this project.

As always, my family—Chris, Joe, Ella, and Judy—thank you for always supporting me in my eccentric projects and understanding when I disappear to pick away at one of my endeavours.

I would like to respectfully acknowledge that I live and work on the island of Ktaqmkuk (Newfoundland), the ancestral and unceded traditional territory of the Beothuck and Mi'kmaq. I acknowledge with respect the diverse histories and cultures of the Beothuck, Mi'kmaq, Innu, and Inuit of this province. As First Peoples have done since time immemorial, I strive to be a responsible steward of the land and to respect the cultures, ceremonies, and traditions of all who call it home. I am committed to listening, learning, and working in a spirit of truth and reconciliation to make a better future for all.

CREDIT: RITCHE PEREZ

About the Author

Heather Barrett, a journalist, storyteller, and international award-winning radio documentary producer, is the co-author, with Xaiver Michael Campbell, of *Black Harbour: Slavery and the Forgotten Histories of Black People in Newfoundland and Labrador* (Boulder Books, 2023). Heather is also a long-time producer and host with the Canadian Broadcasting Corporation.

Born and raised in St. John's, Newfoundland and Labrador, where she lives with her family, Heather holds a Bachelor of Music from Memorial University of Newfoundland and a Master of Arts in Journalism from Western University in London, Ontario. When she is not telling stories, Heather is an avid knitter and an avid runner, but not at the same time.